THE LITTLE ORATORY

THE LITTLE ORATORY

A Beginner's Guide to Praying in the Home

by David Clayton and
Leila Marie Lawler

illustrations by David Clayton
and Deirdre M. Folley

SOPHIA INSTITUTE PRESS
Manchester, New Hampshire

Except where otherwise noted, biblical references in this book are taken from the Revised Standard Version of the Bible, copyright 1952 (2nd edition, 1971) by the Division of Christian Education of the National Council of the Churches of Christ in the United States of America. Used by permission. All rights reserved.

Sophia Institute Press
Box 5284, Manchester, NH 03108
1-800-888-9344
www.SophiaInstitute.com

Sophia Institute Press® is a registered trademark of Sophia Institute.

Library of Congress Cataloging-in-Publication Data
Clayton, David (David N.)
 The little oratory : a beginner's guide to praying in the home / by David Clayton and Leila M. Lawler.
   pages cm
  ISBN 978-1-62282-176-1 (pbk. : alk. paper) 1. Prayer—Catholic Church. 2. Families—Religious life. 3. Spiritual life—Catholic Church. I. Lawler, Leila M. II. Title.
  BV210.3.C56 2014
  249—dc23
                                                          2013045612

First printing

CONTENTS

Appendices

About the Images

———— ❧ ————

At the back of this book are eight color plates of sacred art. These can be easily removed and are a standard size for affordable mounting and framing for your prayer corner. Each is a reproduction of a painting by David Clayton.

If you want a larger image, you may download and print one in color from this site: www. SophiaInstitute.com/LittleOratory. You will also find several images of original Gothic illuminations from the *Westminster Psalter*, all the other images of sacred art included in this book as line drawings, and several more that are not in the book. You may like to print these to use as models to copy if you are teaching (or learning) to draw iconographic and Gothic-style images. They also make beautiful coloring pages.

You can commission work from David Clayton through http://thewayofbeauty.org.

The other illustrations, which are interspersed throughout the text, are by Deirdre M. Folley. You can commission work from her through www.deirdrefolley.com.

Consult chapter 3 for suggestions about the choice and placement of the main elements of the artwork in your home.

THE COLOR PRINTS

1. **A crucifixion in the early Gothic style**. This Franciscan cross, an image of the suffering Christ, can be the centerpiece of your little oratory. The original hangs in the chapel of Thomas More College of Liberal Arts in Manchester, New Hampshire.

2. and 3. **Images of our Lady and our Lord**. One is Gothic (with the blue shawl) and one iconographic in style.

4. and 5. These are images of **Christ in glory**. One is Christ sitting on His heavenly throne, with the four Evangelists (Matthew is symbolized by the angel, Mark by the lion, Luke by the ox, and John by the eagle) carrying the Word off to the four corners of the world. The second image is called a Mandylion (or Image of Edessa), the face of the Savior on a cloth; in the West there is a similar tradition of Veronica's veil. Tradition holds that the original was not painted by man: the icon was created when Veronica's veil was taken to Edessa, where a miraculous healing occurred. Then artists copied this original.

You may like to put the remaining images in your little oratory or elsewhere in your home.

6. **The Visitation**. This image is based on the late-twelfth-century English illuminated manuscript the *Westminster Psalter*. It depicts Our Lady's meeting with her cousin Elizabeth.

7. **St. Michael slaying the dragon**. The heavenly drama is played out and won eternally. John Paul II exhorted the faithful to revive the tradition of praying for the intercession of the powerful archangel Michael against the forces of darkness. You can hear a wonderful musical setting for the prayer to St. Michael at the website The Way of Beauty: http://thewayofbeauty.org. The sheet music is also available.

8. **King David**. This image is based on an original from the *Westminster Psalter*. King David was the composer of the Psalms, the book that St. Thomas Aquinas declared "contains all of theology."

THE LINE DRAWINGS

DO WE WRITE OR PAINT ICONS?

A note from David Clayton:

When people discuss icons, some insist that the word *paint* is inappropriate and that one ought to talk about *writing* icons. The reason usually given is that we are visually representing the Word of God, and words are written, not painted.

My study of the issue reveals that the Greek verb used to describe the creation of an icon can be translated as either "to paint" or "to write." The Orthodox themselves are not unified on this matter. Most of those I know who are painters of icons don't really care what you call what they do. For example, my teacher, who is very well respected in the Eastern Orthodox world, said he thought it was "a bit precious" to insist on using the verb "to write" in English.

To my mind, if I am creating a work by applying paint with a paintbrush, that is called painting. It doesn't lower the status of an icon by considering it to have been painted rather than written.

Regardless of what you choose to call the art of making an icon, there is no justification for applying one word to icons and another to the other authentic liturgical traditions of sacred art, for instance, the Gothic and the Baroque. The iconographic style is not inherently superior to other liturgical forms, and there are no writings of Church Fathers that even suggest it (although you might not believe it to talk to some people today).

What Is This Book About?

We have tried with this book to answer a very basic question: How can I be Catholic in between the times when I am worshipping in church; and especially, how can I be Catholic at home? In short, how can I live a unified life of faith?

For some people, the answer is part of their upbringing. As their parents did, so do they. You might call this a collective memory—a way of doing that everyone seems to know, passed along the generations. In later years this collective memory is lost, it seems.

At least for us, your authors, the explanation for our own journey is that neither of us grew up in a Catholic family. We are both converts. As we grew in our faith (quite independently—we didn't meet until relatively recently), we realized that we were missing practical knowledge. You might say we were missing a Catholic culture—a life lived in harmony with the Faith.

We (separately, unbeknownst to each other) set out to discover these things for ourselves. We read our *Catechism*, books on theology and apologetics, and Church documents and tried to find out as much as we could about the Liturgy, prayers, and devotions (especially to Mary, the Blessed Mother) and how all of this might be applied in a family setting. This was helpful, but we felt that it would have been even better if we had found someone to show us exactly what to do. The obvious thing was to ask (or surreptitiously observe) other Catholics. To our surprise, we found that very few could tell us anything. Even those brought up in Catholic homes were as mystified and ignorant as we were (or so it seemed—because it might be that we ourselves were not looking in the right places or listening to our friends when they tried to show us what to do—and that is part of the journey as well; sometimes we aren't spiritually mature enough to grasp what is in front of us).

If you try reading how-to books on Catholic life, or even well meant prayer handbooks, you will often be presented with a bewildering smorgasbord of prayers, devotions, duties, and commandments. These, although they are supposed to help in life and show how to get to heaven, seem more like a burden. How does anyone manage to fit in daily Mass, the Divine Office, the Rosary, the Divine Mercy Chaplet, the Jesus Prayer, devotion to the Sacred Heart, and everything else—on top of a family life?

As we found out about these things, rather than being excited about each new discovery, we became increasingly overwhelmed by the sheer volume of prayers we were supposed to be saying. The main result was an increasing sense of guilt, as the list of prayers we were failing to say lengthened.

But surely this is the opposite of what it ought to be. Isn't all of this to help us through life rather than to make life more difficult? Christ told us that His yoke is easy and His burden is light (Matt. 11:30). Either this is true or it isn't.

In the end, we found the truth of Jesus' precept that the Christian life comes down to two things: love of God and love of neighbor (Matt. 22:37–39). At the center of the first is our worship at Mass; the center of the second is built in the home and radiates outward.

This book focuses on uniting the two by extending the Eucharistic worship into the heart of the home in the "little oratory," which becomes the visible sign of everything else. The little oratory—prayer table, icon corner, or even dining room table—isn't only a physical place; it's a way of thinking that simplifies everything. The spiritual place in the home mirrors the "interior palace" of our soul, as St. Teresa of Avila called it. At the same time, it allows us to live the liturgical life of the Church. If we get this right, it orders the rest and brings peace.

Gradually (again, independently) we worked out how to put things into practice. Regardless of how humble you think your family is in comparison with the ideal family of faithful prayer in your mind, the truth remains that your family and your home are the basis of culture. If they are rooted in worship, the culture will be affected. If not, well, the culture will still be affected, but not as positively. Thus, in giving you the tools to practice your faith in the heart of your home, we hope that what we offer here might contribute to a renewed Catholic culture.

Our discovery is that what Christ told us is indeed true: His burden is light—and to a degree that we had not previously imagined possible. As a result, and despite our poor efforts (and only when writing a book about the subject do we feel the force of this "*poor*"), our homes have become places of greater love and peace. We hope that our experiences can help you.

We are ordinary Catholics, so if we can do it, so can you. God, we believe, understands our failings and supports us and completes our efforts on our behalf. The adage "Pray for rain and dig for water" applies very well here, we think!

God knows that we cannot pray on our own. He sends His Spirit to help us. As St. Paul tells us: "The Spirit comes to the aid of our weakness; when we do not know what prayer to offer, to pray as we ought, the Spirit himself intercedes for us, with groans beyond all utterance: and God, who can read our hearts, knows well what the Spirit's intent is; for indeed it is according to the mind of God that he makes intercession for the saints" (Rom. 8:26–27, Knox Bible).

Citing St. Paul, Pope Emeritus Benedict XVI writes: "The Spirit of Christ becomes the strength of our 'weak' prayer, the light of our 'dimmed' prayer, the focus of our 'dry' prayer, giving us true inner freedom, teaching us to live by facing our trials, in the certainty we are not alone … This freedom manifests itself in the 'fruits of the Spirit' which are 'love, joy, peace, patience, kindness, generosity, faithfulness, gentleness, self-control.'"[1]

HOW TO READ THIS BOOK

We have written this book so that each part stands on its own. This means that you can dip in and read for ten minutes or look something up quickly if you like. The heart of this book deals with making a little oratory and perhaps praying all or part of the Liturgy of the Hours there with your family (chapters 3 through 9; you can certainly feel free to go straight there and get started).

At the same time, we have tried to present a single, integrated, flowing text, with, perhaps,

some inevitable repetition. But that's how our Faith is: no sooner do you feel that you have grasped one aspect of it than you see how it relates to another and, indeed, is contained in it. So, naturally, each section will reflect and illuminate what came before and point to what comes next. We have included some longer sections that explain things a little more deeply.

There are many aspects of the Faith, and even of the Domestic Church (the life of the Faith in the home), that we have skimmed lightly over or entirely omitted. Another book would be necessary to go into the particulars of a full treatment of the Mass (including family attendance and how to achieve it); the devotion of frequent Confession; the theology of marriage; many wonderful devotions; family meals and family fasts; a long look at the practice of charity; and no doubt, many other topics. It is our hearty recommendation that you often consult the *Catechism of the Catholic Church* for a full, beautifully integrated treatment of Catholic life and beliefs.

We've tried to have as our organizing principle the home altar, the icon corner, or, as the *Catechism* calls it, the little oratory. Sometimes we've strayed a bit far from it, but in general, we've tried to keep our vision limited to what this corner of our home can teach us about living the Faith.

In the chapter on the Liturgy of the Hours, we present a range of choices for using the psalter (the book of psalms). The one you

---

[1] Benedict XVI, public address, May 16, 2012, St. Peter's Square; quoted in David Kerr, "Pope Outlines Power of the Holy Spirit in Prayer," Catholic News Agency, May 16, 2012.

choose will depend on your individual preferences; whether you are praying publicly (in a parish church, for example) or privately in your home; and, for practical reasons, what version those around you are using (because perhaps they will be instructing you, or the person leading is a priest who uses a certain version). The good standing of versions can change over time and in particular areas and can depend on your own situation. For example, some people belong to the Western Rite, others to the Eastern Rite, and so on. We encourage you to seek guidance from those in authority in your area if you have any doubts about the validity of the psalter that you would like to use.

However you use this book, we hope that you will be inspired to continue with your own reflections; above all, we hope that, by getting a grasp of the underlying principles we've tried to set forth, you start to develop your own personal ways of living your faith in the home. After all, only Sacred Tradition is immutable. Human traditions change and develop, are lost and recovered. Perhaps you will be able to work things out better than we have done and write a better book for the next generation!

THE LITTLE ORATORY

The Christian Life

God became man so that man
might become God.

St. Athanasius,
On the Incarnation, 54:3

This book is about making a little oratory —a little sacred space—in your home and praying there. Many people who don't have a little oratory have great faith. We ourselves didn't know about this way of expressing faith for most of our lives. Really, it is just an outward manifestation of the simple truth that God wants to be with us. He is Emmanuel, *God with us.*

We want to be with *God,* but often we don't see how to do so, in practice. Once we acknowledge our need for God, the most difficult challenge we face seems to be reconciling our human, fallen nature with the demands of faith. When we are so distracted, so fractured, and have so many reasonable demands made on our time (leaving aside the demands not in accord with reason), we can get discouraged.

Although our prayer life, our family life, and our work life should be in harmony, each one deepening and enriching the other, in practice they often seem in competition with each other. We want to raise our children well, be hospitable, and pray. We understand very well that we are all called to love God in union with Him.

In particular, the world we live in—the material world with all its multiplicity, so full of joy and goodness, but also so intractable and often violent—seems to be definitively sundered from the world we wish to inhabit—the spiritual world of peace and union with God.

It seems that we cannot reach the heights. And it's true. We cannot. Millennia of desire have passed, proving this. Man cannot heal the rift between earth and heaven. He cannot grasp heaven to bring it down to earth, and yet on earth he is bound to stay.

The Good News is that instead, God sent His Son to heal the breach. By Christ's Incarnation, it has been done—heaven and earth meet in the Word. "The Incarnation is therefore the mystery of the wonderful union of the divine and human natures in the one person of the Word" (*Catechism of the Catholic Church* [CCC] 483). He had to become a man, fully divine in nature but fully human as well, in order to bring about this unity, which was then sealed with His death and Resurrection. The process of redemption begins at the moment Jesus is conceived in His mother's womb.

By God's grace we are raised to something higher than our human nature until we share in God's divine nature. We relate first to a man, Jesus Christ. But because Jesus Christ is both man and God, through this personal relationship we become children of God.

This is why Christianity is a faith rooted in the person, Jesus Christ, who is both God

and man. Through this relationship, we enter into the mystery of the Trinity, the dynamic of love between the three persons: Father, Son, and Holy Spirit. All the sacraments and the commandments of the Church—indeed, the Church herself—are directed toward this relationship with God.

Thus, Christian life consists of a public, visible life of worship of God in the church; fellowship with other Christians; service to one's neighbor; evangelization. And then there is the inner, invisible spiritual life of the Christian, which is less visible: the inner spiritual life of prayer and devotions, fasting and almsgiving.

Jesus is the Light of the World. The possibility of living a life of integrated faith is a path lit by this Light. It's not a matter of tension, of conflict. It's a matter of simply being present to this moment when God united divinity and humanity, spirit and flesh, in the Person of His Son.

SHINING WITH THE LIGHT OF CHRIST

But was it a moment? How do we keep the "moment" of the Incarnation, so tied to history, so rooted in a particular time and place long past, before our eyes, so to speak?

Look at the drawing of an early fifteenth-century icon of the Transfiguration at the beginning of this chapter (see the full version at www.SophiaInstitute.com/LittleOratory).

The composition of this dramatic icon puts the radiant Christ in the center. The Old Testament prophets Moses and Elijah, who bow reverently, stand on either side of Him. Peter, on the bottom left, is shown talking to Christ, and all the disciples are manifestly disoriented by what they are seeing and hearing (see Matt. 17:1–7).

Jean Corbon, who wrote the beautiful section on prayer for the *Catechism of the Catholic Church*, describes in *The Wellspring of Worship* how this pivotal moment points not only to Christ's Transfiguration but also to our own, through our participation in the Sacred Liturgy, the Mass.

It is by means of the Liturgy, he says, that the Church becomes the "sacrament of communion between God and man." As members of the Mystical Body of Christ, we partake of the divine nature, becoming "God as much as God becomes man" (Maximus the Confessor). Do you see the connection with the Incarnation? The Eucharist is the continuation through time of the moment of the Incarnation, the means by which we, two millennia later, reach back to the enfleshment of the Word, becoming part of it. The True Presence of Christ is His *whole* presence—every bit of Him, from His conception to His Resurrection, including His life in union with the Trinity in Heaven.

We can't see this light unless we are pure, for sin clouds the inner vision of our spirit.

The disciples, depicted in the icon as quite stricken and of diminished proportion, can see the transfigured Christ and hear the voice of the Father on this occasion because they are becoming pure, symbolized by their going up with Christ to Mount Tabor, up to the heights. Their posture is prone, but they *are* in the heights. In this life, we too, by degrees, through our participation in the Liturgy, humbly ascend the holy mountain.

For Corbon, there is a threefold manifestation taking place here: first, the revealing of Christ; second, the purification of heart that enables us to see and grasp the truth; and third and finally, "if we are given the gift of 'believing in his name' and if we have received 'power to become sons of God'" (John 1:12), Jesus sends us into the world as He Himself was sent by His Father. His Spirit gives us a new birth in order that His glory may be manifested to others through us and others, in turn, may be transformed into the body of the Lord. This final extension of the life-giving light—evangelization, in fact—is the reality that is the Body of Christ, bringing into communion the scattered children of God. Progress on the path to heaven is a personal transformation through an ever-deepening participation in the life of the Incarnate God.

If we consent in prayer to be flooded by the river of life, our entire being will be transformed: we will become trees of life and be increasingly able to produce the fruit of the Spirit: we will love with the very Love that is our God ... This process is the drama of divinization in which the mystery of the lived liturgy is brought to completion in each Christian. (Corbon)

So do we really shine with the light of holiness? Do we live as if there is an earthly manifestation of light? Have we ever seen a saint shining like the transfigured Christ? If Corbon is right, then surely one might expect to see at least the occasional halo at the grocery store or a faint light of partial divinization when the lights go down in the movie theater. Are saints so hard to come by?

An Orthodox monk, a teacher of iconography, tells a story: Two saints met, and as they spoke to each other, each saw the other shining with a halo of uncreated light. They were both amazed and later described what they had seen to a third party. On hearing the tale from each of them, the third person realized what was happening—that each was a holy and pure man, unaware of his own light, but seeing the light in the other. The third person, who knew both, could not see the light in either.

This suggests that perhaps we have seen saintly people without knowing it. What hope is there for us? If only the holy and pure can see others who are holy, where does that leave us poor sinners? It seems like a supernatural paradox of discouraging proportions. But it's Christ in us who will see Christ in others.

For this light that transfigures both work and the created thing that work shapes is the light of communion. Like the Eucharistic liturgy, the Eucharist as lived out in daily life is crowned by communion. At bottom, it is the absence of this communion that is at the root of injustices in the workplace, with its alienating structures, and of disorders in the economy. The liturgy does not do away with the need for our inventiveness in dealing with these problems. However, it does something even better: since it is not a structure but the Breath of Spirit, it is prophetic; it discerns, it challenges;

it spurs creativity and is translated into actions. It cries out for justice and is the agent of peace. (Corbon)

THE LITURGY

Thus, we see that it is the Liturgy that provides the key to a unified life. When someone does something beautifully, we often use the word *graceful* to describe it. This is an appropriate word, for we cannot hope to fulfill our calling without God's grace. This is why it starts with prayer and all prayer should be ordered to the highest and most powerful form of prayer, the Sacred Liturgy, which is the public worship of the Church. The *Catechism* tells us that the word *liturgy* originally meant a "service in the name of/on behalf of the people" and in the Christian tradition came to mean the "participation of the People of God in the work of God" (CCC 1069). Its most common usage today is in reference to the public worship of the Church—with the Mass and the Liturgy of the Hours at its foundation—and that is the way we will use it in this book.

Some will not have heard of the Liturgy of the Hours, and so it may be a surprise to learn that, after the Mass, of which it is an extension, the Liturgy of the Hours (also called the Divine Office) is the most powerful and effective prayer there is. It is the God-given worship of the Church, firmly rooted in the ancient worship of the Jews, and it is offered at various times of the day in order to sanctify the day and project the grace of the Eucharist through all the hours.

The Liturgy is the highest form of prayer. It is a supernatural step into the Mystical Body of Christ, His Church, and our mystical participation in the loving dynamic of the Trinity. When we pray the Liturgy, we do what Christ does in loving relationship with the other persons of the Trinity. We pray to the Father, through the Son, in the Spirit; and in doing so, we receive all that the Son receives—that is, a love described by the *Catechism* as "the great love" with which the Father loves us in His Son that is "lived and internalized by all prayer at all times in the Spirit" (CCC 1073; cf. Eph. 6:18).

By this means we participate in God's divine nature: "God put us in the world to know, to love, and to serve Him, and so to come to paradise. Beatitude makes us 'partakers of the divine nature' and of eternal life. With beatitude man enters into the glory of Christ and into the joy of the Trinitarian life" (CCC 1721).

THE PRIVILEGE OF UNION

This vision is an extraordinary privilege that encompasses the cave of Bethlehem and the highest mountain of paradise. It is difficult to imagine what this would be like exactly; except that it must be good and that there cannot be any greater gift, for there is nothing greater than God Himself. It is the happiness that all of us seek.

The *Catechism* tells us that each of us has planted within us a desire for happiness that can alone be satisfied by God. Quoting St. Augustine and St. Thomas, it tells us, "We all want to live happily; in the whole human race there is no one who does not assent to this proposition, even before it is fully articulated. How is it, then, that I seek you, Lord? Since in seeking you, my God, I seek a happy life, let me seek you so that my soul may live, for my body draws life from my soul and my soul draws life from you. God alone satisfies" (CCC 1718).

IS HAPPINESS ATTAINABLE?

It is important for us to know that this state of happiness is something that is attainable. And not just in the future—it is something that we can experience today. The Christian life is not simply a waiting game in which we patiently bear misery until we die and hope

that when we get there, we will qualify to move across the great divide and experience something better in the next life. Although we cannot fully experience this heavenly joy until the next life, we *can* experience it by degrees in this life, through the earthly Liturgy: "In the earthly Liturgy we share in a foretaste of that heavenly liturgy which is celebrated in the Holy City of Jerusalem toward which we journey as pilgrims" (*Sacrosanctum Concilium* 8).

Our progress along this road is marked not only by a passage of time, moving toward the future end of our lives here on earth; but also by personal gradual transformation in holiness, a real change. Almost despite ourselves, we become better people; each more like the person we ought to be. Without our quite knowing how, our lives become a clearer sign, directing others more strongly to the source of this holiness, God. In fact, we become His children.

Pope Benedict XVI called the path the *via pulchritudinis*—the Way of Beauty. We share this joy with others when beauty radiates from us and others see it in us. It calls to them, and they are drawn to the source of our joy, so that it can be theirs too. This current life is a joyful pilgrimage in which we move toward heaven, continuously inviting others to join us on that road in fellowship. It is an inexhaustible well. It is never drained, no matter how many draw from it or how much each draws.

To the degree that each part of our life will support and complement every other and all are ordered to our ultimate goal, our lives will be beautiful. According to St. Thomas Aquinas, one of the essential attributes of beauty is *due proportion*, which means that all parts are in harmony with each other. Another attribute of beauty is *integrity*, which means that the overall purpose of the thing is in harmony with what it is meant to be, which for the Christian is the love of God. The final attribute is *clarity*— it must be radiant and perceptible by others. When people see a life well lived, they are drawn by its beauty and then beyond to the source to which it points, and to which that life is ordered: God.

This is not to deny the struggles and problems that every single one of us experiences, but rather to offer us something that transcends them. We are given grace to deal with any suffering we are asked to endure. Through God's grace, although the trials of life may still be present, Christian joy surpasses them. It offers a solace that overpowers all and places all suffering in a new light.

This Christian joy in suffering is seen at its height in the joy of the martyrs. We aren't martyrs—at least not yet! Nevertheless, we, the authors, and you, the reader, *have* had ups and downs. We've felt fear and insecurity about the future, the sense of regret over actions of the past, isolation as a result of estrangement from God due to our own sins, and the ordinary rejections and ill treatment by others. There is probably cause for great unhappiness in every

life—or blessed indeed is the life that has little of it. But life rooted in the Liturgy is a source of joy that overcomes these everyday trials—and great ones. God gives the grace.

Each of us has a personal calling from God, which is our unique part to play in the building of an earthly liturgical city that is a foretaste of the heavenly liturgical city, the New Jerusalem.

So here is the point: the happy life is the good life; and the good life is the liturgical life, which is to say, a life in union with the living God.

EVANGELIZATION

"Evangelism is one beggar telling another where to find bread" (D. T. Niles).

It's only natural to want to share the Good News—the Word made flesh, the Transfiguration on the mountain, the Bread of Life, the rescue from sin—with others. There's another natural response, however, which is to worry that it seems puffed up or somehow proud to presume to tell another what to do and whom to worship. But listen: if we think of ourselves as beggars who have had the good fortune to find a generous bakery, well, then the selfishness of not sharing the news becomes obvious.

Yet it's clear that simply giving someone the information (perhaps handing him a booklet or offering a program of some sort) lacks a certain holy finesse. Sure, if the person—the other beggar (we're all beggars here)—is hungry enough, it might work. But only because of God's goodness, not because that is the way we're meant to share the Good News.

To continue this image of the beggars, isn't it better for the one to accompany the other along the road? Isn't it better to talk along the way of all sorts of things, not just the terrible condition we find ourselves in? Maybe even sharing a funny story, or walking along in companionable silence, is what fits the occasion.

Best of all is when we make a home, humble as it is, and can invite others into its warmth. Hospitality, in fact, is a true form of sharing God's love. Even angels appreciate it, we're told (Heb. 13:2)!

Our Lord was born into a family. The family is God's plan for the world—His divine plan, conceived in the very beginning, to be a way of beauty and of spreading His word. The special place of prayer at home, the family oratory (*oratory* means "house of prayer") is a powerhouse of grace by which our family may be nourished spiritually and thus be able to transform the world through prayer, proclamation of the gospel, and charity. That sounds grand, but it is really very simple and humble, like the Holy Family itself.

With this book, we are interested in reviving the little oratory, as the *Catechism* calls it (CCC 2691)—prayer table, home altar, or icon corner—in the home. It's an almost lost tradition that can be a simple and beautiful bridge between these two places—home and church—for the sake of the family's life of faith—and consequently for this whole project which is the life of the Christian.

The Family and the Home

*Only by praying together with their children
can a father and mother — exercising their
royal priesthood — penetrate the innermost
depths of their children's hearts and leave an
impression that the future events in their lives
will not be able to efface.*

John Paul II, *Familiaris Consortio*

When we read the first two chapters of Genesis in the Bible, we learn how fundamental to God's plan for creation the family is. In fact, the family *is the plan*. In light of the New Testament, there is no other plan! God sent His Son to redeem fallen man, and the redemption gets us back to these beginnings again. Pope John Paul II explains that in the Gospel of Matthew, Jesus insists that any modifications of the plan for the family be swept away — that we return to "the beginning" with His teaching.

The beginning is this: the first covenant that God made with Adam and Eve, telling them to be fruitful and multiply. He gave them to each other in marriage, saying, "For this reason a man shall leave his father and mother and be joined to his wife" (Matt. 19:5). He gave all of humanity this "unity of the two" (as John Paul II calls it), the "two become one flesh," a unity that mysteriously unfolds into the gift of new life, a child.

A loving home of our own is a fundamental need embedded in our human nature. It's rooted in the original plan that God has for man, which He lays forth in Genesis when He creates man in His image. He creates them male and female and institutes the covenant of marriage, which, in the unity of the two persons, can find adequate expression of love only in the flesh of another person, the child whom they beget.

This community is human; it has bodily needs and those of the soul. This embodiment means, among other things, that the family must have a place where it dwells, and that place is its home.

A family has a home; the home is the place where the family lives. In the beginning, this home and the earthly paradise were one and the same! Home was truly a garden sanctuary.

Later, after the fall, the home needed to be a shelter. But while necessarily being a physical structure of some kind, the home remained so much more. The sheltering place where the family carries out its mission ("to guard, reveal, and communicate love," in John Paul's words) has a dimension to it that

is very real, retained from its beginnings — this dimension of being a sanctuary that mirrors the intimate life of God Himself. God ratified all this by becoming Incarnate in the bosom of a family, in a home.

THE HOME

The home, you might say, ought to be a little Eden on earth; or better, because we are now redeemed, a little bit of heaven. It's truly, as John Paul points out, the one place where everyone is accepted for who he is rather than for what he does or what he contributes, and that alone makes it very restful. At the same time, the family is uniquely suited to the development of the human person. A person develops his potential by means of the nourishment of love.

Perhaps you yourself have experienced, or have heard stories, of a person stepping inside a Catholic church without knowing anything of the real presence — Body, Blood, soul, and divinity — of our Lord in the tabernacle. Yet, despite any preconceived ideas about what the church holds, the person nevertheless senses some sort of otherly presence.

There is a hush, yes; there is the sanctuary candle, yes. There is an undeniable mystique to the place. But each of those elements only indicates beyond itself something more, something greater than a sum of its parts—something that, when the person encounters it, makes him long to be a part of it.

This sense of a mysterious quality can be found in the home as well. When we enter people's homes, we catch a whiff of their essence, of who they are, and of the divine. This whiff may not always be completely wholesome! Sometimes a home conveys the disorder within: a lack of unity, neglect, unhappiness. Imagine a home (such as one encountered by one of your authors) where there is a terrible disorder: utter chaos within, the mother with a drink in her hand at an early hour, the obvious distress of her children. You might have conversed previously outside, while the kids rode their bikes, not having known anything was wrong. You might have had no hint of this situation before entering the home. But once inside, you felt it.

That kind of terrible disorder could be due to unimaginable imbalances and abuse. There is no way of knowing why the center is so far off or how things came to spin so badly out of orbit. The disorder certainly is not to be confused with simple messiness or normal signs of life, with children and family members in general who, taken up with their interests and vitality, haven't gotten around to tidying up. In fact, the paradox is that sometimes the neatest homes are the coldest, and often those with a certain lived-in feel are the most welcoming.

The home reveals so much.

HOSPITALITY

Truly, families humbly living the mission of love (even if they are not particularly religious) have the characteristic of creating a home. It's as strong as if a lamp is lit, quietly proclaiming the presence of the hidden sacrament of love to the inhabitants and to others.

The spirit of that home—that particular, unique home—is palpable to the visitor, just as the visitor feels something real upon entering a church. The stranger goes away taking a piece of it in his heart, being affirmed in his own unique calling. A person doesn't lose his identity upon being welcomed into a real, loving home; rather, he finds something in himself he didn't know before. The experience of being in a happy home draws forth love in its inhabitants and in its guests.

It's good to think a little about what hospitality is, for today a person can stay in a hotel very easily, and it's just as easy never to entertain guests. It was not always so. For most of the ages of humanity, anyone traveling could easily be that "stranger" in need of shelter. If a family didn't offer refuge, that traveler could be left out in the cold.

The willingness to allow people into the sanctuary of our home is corporal charity—care for their bodily needs, such as hunger—that can be elevated to providing a spiritual sanctuary as well. The home should be a place where a person can find rest, yes, and food. But it should also be a place where friends and family can gather to enjoy each other's company—to relax and just have fun. And it should be a place to share the Faith and our devotion as well.

A SCHOOL OF VIRTUE AND A DOMESTIC CHURCH

In the home, the family—simply as a function of what the family is, as instituted by God at the beginning of creation—has two utterly important roles: to be a school of virtue and to be a domestic church. You might say that the family lives out these roles without thinking too much about them—with the intuition of love.

1. The future of humanity passes by way of the family, a school of virtue.

To understand the depth of these missions entrusted to the family, let's consider: It's obvious that a child comes into the world needing to learn everything! The child has to learn about the existence of reality itself—of something beyond his own bodily needs—a universe waiting to be apprehended, grasped, submitted to, conquered. The child must develop in every possible way that a human can develop—intellectually, psychologically, physically, emotionally, aesthetically.

Yet as a child, he must first be loved, so that he can attend this "school of the existence of reality" with an open heart. Even the first act of the mother, which is tenderly cradling her child at her breast, is formative.

As soon as we start to think about this, we realize that far from benefiting from lectures on "The Good" or "The True" or even "How to Behave," the child can really learn virtue only in a setting where he can be nurtured and corrected by those who are simultaneously struggling themselves to grow in virtue and who treat him with the warm affection only family bonds can supply.

All members of the family, each according to his own gift, have the grace and responsibility of building, day by day, the communion of persons, making the family "a school of deeper humanity" (*Familiaris Consortio* 59): this happens where there is care and love for the little ones, the sick, the aged; where there is mutual service every day; when there is a sharing of goods and of joys and of sorrows.

2. The Domestic Church

With Aristotle we can define *virtue* as the *habit* of doing good. The best way for a person to learn real virtue is by living with good people who love him. The best way to learn to love God is to grow up with habits that are grounded in ritual, prayer, and holiness. And that is because there is an aspect to learning in general that requires not only active teaching but also silence and the room to acknowledge mystery.

The family is where each child discovers what John Paul calls that "first expression of man's inner truth," namely, prayer and devotion. His habits are formed in a way that intuitively suits his development and temperament—simply by being known and loved in his family. The developing child needs a setting where this expression can unfold.

JESUS HIMSELF WAS BORN IN A HOME, SANCTIFYING IT

Jesus Himself was born into a family, which is of the greatest significance for us as we think about what *our* homes should be like. The Lord of the universe, one supposes, could have come to redeem mankind in some other way—by emerging fully grown from behind a bush, or

perhaps by entering the material world as he left it, in a cloud of unknowing.

But instead, God Himself chose to embrace the stuff of which we are made in the most definitive way possible: by being conceived in the womb of a mortal woman and by growing in the same fashion as every other person on earth, including living in a home. The Redemption began in a physical place, and that means that the womb, and later the home itself was also a sanctuary, a tabernacle.

Although it goes without saying that the home of Mary, Jesus, and Joseph was modest, it might be worth considering its specific characteristics. As soon as we ask the question, "Was it beautiful?" we know the answer. Yes, of course. It was beautiful.

Thinking about the nature of the home we want—the shelter that is more than a shelter, the sanctuary where those who enter feel a presence and take away with them love, we see that it also must be beautiful, however humble it is.

Thus, we can start to consider the family as a school of beauty as well as a school of virtue.

In fact, the Way of Beauty, you might say, is the precursor for the Way of Goodness (how the good leads us to God, who is Good) and the Way of Truth (how the truth leads us to God, who is Truth). Beauty is fittingness, sweet order, and harmony. (That is so even when it is depicting evil or ugliness, by the way. Beauty can't betray itself.)

We call something beautiful when it is pleasing to the eyes, and in fact all the senses can delight in the perception of something good (although we might not use the word *beautiful* for taste, for example). A child begins to learn, through family life, that there are good and bad smells; how certain textiles feel under his fingertips; what constitutes lovely images and what images are displeasing. He is enchanted by the light of a candle. Sounds shape his world: the way birds tune up in spring, even when the snow is still on the ground; kind voices in happy conversation in the distance; the hum of machines restoring order to the household. Music especially opens up a whole world of beauty: sweet lullabies, wonderful tunes passed down using homey instruments available to all, beloved Christmas carols sung every year. The child's environment can be an education in beauty for him.

It was in homes that the first altars, dedicated and blessed, were established, on which were celebrated the Eucharistic Liturgy. Early mosaics from the fifth and sixth centuries, as seen, for example, at Sant'Appollinare or San Vitale in Ravenna, portray a home altar at which people stood and on which people placed offerings. This altar was distinct from the dining table, which is shown as a lower, often semicircular piece of furniture, with people sitting or reclining (as was the custom) while eating.

Today, even though our church is separate from our home, there is no way we can have moved beyond the importance of the Domestic Church—no way that we could think that the home has become unnecessary to a full articulation of faith. A child still must be raised. The sanctuary lamp must still burn in our hearts and in the community of love, the home.

DEVELOPING THE DOMESTIC CHURCH

The thought behind our exploration of all the details of the little oratory in this book is to take this further, to develop this side of family life as a "domestic church." We want to encourage traditional and personal ways to make a lovely space in our home that is both a space set apart, church-like, and a space that apotheosizes the beauty that we try to express in the rest of the home.

(We should be clear that we are not advocating "home church" or any sort of replacement for the Divine Liturgy, the normal celebration of which, for families, will be at the parish church. Scripture and Tradition set down the criteria for worship, and we couldn't be more devoted to it—it's the center and root of everything, as we have said. Without the ordained priesthood, the celebration of the Mass, and the gathering of the faithful, Christianity would not be what Christ established.)

In Eastern Christian traditions, the icon corner is the place in the home where the blessed icons can have pride of place. The corner provides a setting for the two-dimensional objects to be in relationship with each other. A shelf provides the spot for a candle and incense, perhaps.

In the West, the importance of statues and freestanding crucifixes makes a table a good choice, and a table can remind us of an altar.

Thus, the home altar developed in various places in different ways. Usually these altars are simple, but not always. In Italy, offerings of bread and pastries are heaped on a St. Joseph table. In Latino homes, nativities are displayed with lavishness and complexity.

East or West, we institute our family rituals and display our precious objects that express our love for the Lord. In the following chapters, we will give you the specifics of how this is done.

For now, let's simply begin to meditate on this reality: that the objective order of truth, beauty, and goodness can be mysteriously expressed in ways unique to our own particular homes. We'll look at beauty (along with a nod to functionality) in the home and then be ready to think about the little oratory—the prayer table, home altar, or icon corner.

SINGLES

Can a home altar exist where there is a single person or a family that is somehow broken or has lost a loved one? Yes, the dwelling place is your home! The physical space you live in must be more than a utilitarian environment in which you go about the business of daily life, taking care of basic needs. You can make it beautiful and warm, practicing hospitality. A single person is encouraged to have a little oratory! A single parent is encouraged to have a little oratory!

Where the single person is struggling to make the home a sanctuary, it might be good to remember that man was made for family life. Go back to Genesis and read what God said at the Creation: It is not good for man to be alone (cf. Gen. 2:18). Even in religious institutions, where the persons are not single but are not married either, the head is called "Mother" or "Father," and life together is given a family air. A single person should take care to make his home a warm, inviting place where a community can form. In our broken world, a family feeling can be offered to those who are lacking real blood ties.

A single person should also consider the vocation of being of service to a family, to help the family, in John Paul's words, "become what they are." In today's world, families are unfortunately stripped to their barest level, blandly labeled "nuclear"—necessary but insufficient in many ways to meet life's challenges. The pressure on mother and father is overwhelming at times. And children often feel the confines of having only their parents to relate to in the family setting. The family can only barely survive, and not really flourish, without the natural extension of grown siblings, grandparents, and aunts and uncles—even honorary—who in the past lightened the load and provided welcome companionship, as well as received it. A single person might be able to help a family make their own prayer table, if the project seems overwhelming to the parents drowning in daily cares.

THE HOME IS A SCHOOL OF BEAUTY

The recognition of beauty moves us to love what we see. We are drawn to it and then beyond to its source, God. To be educated in beauty from an early age—with that education of love that the home offers—tends to incline us to serve God and our fellow man with love. The result for those individuals who follow this path of beauty is joy.

The intellect has two modes: the step-by-step fashion of working things out with effort; and also the way of insight, of intuition. Suddenly, we grasp the matter, whatever it may be, all at once, and we say, "Oh, I see!"

When we apprehend beauty, we do so intuitively. So a formation in beauty develops our intuitive capacity. We can start to rely on our new intuition as well as our deductive reasoning when faced with a choice, allowing ourselves to be led by the "kindly light" referred to by John Henry Newman in his famous hymn.

The artist finds that habitually praying with visual imagery nourishes his art; he finds that his art nourishes his prayer. The habit of praying with visual imagery will develop our instinct for what is beautiful, even if we don't happen to be an artist.

True creativity is the ability to create in accord with this pattern of beauty. We can see the answers to problems that previously might have baffled us. We can spot the omissions and deviations from the pattern of beauty. We see how to complete or correct the picture. The liturgical life therefore stimulates and forms the creative.

Because the family is where the child is first formed in what constitutes the beautiful, which in turn relates to the good and the true, it is no exaggeration to say that the images we choose for our prayer in the home can have a profound effect on the culture and, ultimately, on the good of others.

EDUCATING OURSELVES IN BEAUTY

Here are some ways to educate ourselves and our children in beauty.

• *Study the beauty of creation (the pattern of heaven reflected in the cosmos).* If we study the work of the Creator, this will help us to make our work participate in the divine beauty that it bears. All children can learn to observe nature by drawing it. When the youngster seems amenable, start with simple but interesting forms that don't require the child to synthesize too much. A landscape is extraordinarily difficult to draw; at the beginning, it seems so complex that it is almost overwhelming. Even drawing a single tree is very difficult, because it presents the problem of how visually to

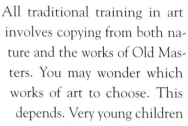

distill thousands of branches and millions of leaves; drawing a single daffodil is a bit easier. So start with still life: a single piece of driftwood or perhaps just three or four simple natural objects such as pebbles or eggs. The goal is as much to take the time to observe and delight in nature as to learn to produce a good painting.

As children progress in their education, they will start to study other aspects of nature. Natural history and science should be seen as different ways of meditation on the order of nature. The mathematics that underpins science, for example, is a language that describes *pattern* as much as *quantity*. In addition to mastering a skill, the person becomes aware of the beauty of the symmetry and order that mathematical operations reflect — simply to delight in it.

• *Study the beauty of the Old Masters — the pattern of heaven as reflected in a liturgical culture.*

All traditional training in art involves copying from both nature and the works of Old Masters. You may wonder which works of art to choose. This depends. Very young children could color in line drawings based on traditional forms (see the resources at the end of this book).

The more sophisticated might try some tonal work on a copy of a Baroque painting. A fruitful exercise is to imitate Gothic or Romanesque illuminated manuscripts, which are line drawings with limited modeling. They are great fun to draw, and most of us in the West seem to relate to them more readily than to Eastern iconographic forms. You don't need to feel bound to sacred imagery. The *Westminster Psalter*, for instance, includes pictures of the everyday life of the time.

Beyond these suggestions, choose any work of art that has withstood the test of time — ideally, several generations. Beauty is timeless; fashion is not. Therefore, train your eye with something that can withstand the vagaries of fashion and transcend its own time — which is more likely to be truly beautiful than something that cannot.

• *Study sacred chant.* Any education in beauty should include chant in all its modes. Modes are different keys that arise from different relative positions of half-tone and whole-tone intervals in an eight-note scale. Modern conventional music has just two modes, called the major and minor keys. Traditional chant is usually considered to have eight modes (or sometimes nine).

Just as with art, the patterns of music impress themselves upon the soul through the musical intervals and harmonious relationships. Accordingly, the essential patterns that the beauty of the cosmos comprises and that ultimately point to God are reflected in a noble but simple way in chant, which is the music par excellence for the Liturgy, as set out in the Church's instruction of sacred music, *Tra le Sollecitudini*, of Pius X.

Most of what we think of as classical and contemporary (but not atonal) music contains only two modes (referred to as the major and the minor keys). If children are exposed to only those forms, no matter how beautiful they may be, they will have a narrower education than if they have exposure to modal music as well.

If, at the center of worship, we keep the modal forms, we will have a more balanced exposure to music. Of course, classical, jazz, folk, and pop music are delightful, each in its own way, in other areas of life. Whatever you find that your children can experience as beautiful, include! Keep in mind that you need to introduce some forms of music sparingly, as they are heavy and cerebral (thinking of much of the later classical period). Apart from chant,

children especially benefit from folk music of whatever style appeals to you, which is as lively and fun for them as for adults.

Many of our readers are not familiar at all with chant, much less comfortable chanting themselves! For those parents who want to learn, we have some ideas as to how you might at least be able to make a very basic start later in this book.

Recent popes have reminded artists that beauty can be so attractive that those who would never go to church otherwise seek it out because of the beauty they find there. Regardless of whether persons have had a formal education in beauty, its power is such that it transforms them by degrees—or suddenly—until hearts are opened up to receive the Word.

The education in beauty that we are describing is not aimed directly at these people, therefore. Rather, it is for those who will be the *creators* of the culture who will subsequently attract the unevangelized. The education in beauty is for those who are already aware of the relationship between truth, beauty, and goodness; that is, perhaps, readers of this book! It is a formation that equips our children to be creators of beauty on behalf of the Church.

HOLY DECORATING

Every home shares some characteristics. Every person has to eat and sleep and recreate. The areas or rooms where these things are done take on their own flavor from the preferences of the members, intentionally or not. We usually think of *decorating* as the way to describe what happens to the environment of the home, but when we consider that the way the home looks is not at all superficial or added on to what the home is, we see that there is something more than decorating going on.

Principles of design

Folks have their own ways of expressing themselves, and we heartily encourage that uniqueness. There are some principles for comfort and design; the idea in mentioning them is that they will enhance your creativity, not stifle it. We think these principles are worth discussing for those who are not used to thinking about decorating in specifically family-oriented and God-oriented terms.

Each room in the house needs to reflect its functionality and the taste of the inhabitants. It's nice to have a small reminder of faith throughout: a crucifix, an image of our Lady. The idea isn't to shock and awe with our religiosity — that would be ultimately counterproductive and not particularly beautiful, since beauty is found in proportion; and in the home, beauty expresses all the aspects of human nature, not only the spiritual. On the other hand, we Christians want to reflect our belief and devotion in every room (and hopefully every area of our life), so it's fitting to have a reminder wherever we are.

Two design notes for any and every room in the house

• *Shelves.* There is hardly a place in the house that isn't enhanced by the use of shelving — either built in or in dressers or hutches — to provide storage and a homey atmosphere. They use space well: because things stored on them are in view, their owner learns to value attractive usefulness, which naturally reduces clutter.

• *Color.* We are including a word about color choices in decorating in case you are about to make some changes. We would rather encourage you to go ahead with your little oratory rather than redecorate first! But if you are choosing paint colors, it might be nice to have your religious art in mind. Very often, choosing color is where people experience the most frustration, especially when it comes to coordinating colors with religious art. As regards the home altar in particular, some colors work better than others in décor.

On the walls and the larger pieces of furniture we suggest that you use soft whites and neutral colors that relate to nature's tones. That way, the art in the little oratory will stand out and not clash with the wall paint. Your love of color may be expressed in textiles and accents so as not to overwhelm a room. Again, don't let things as they are prevent you from forging ahead with your prayer-table plans.

Master bedroom

In every home, there are sleeping areas. Mother and father's room should never be made the repository for laundry, boxes, and other detritus. On the contrary, it should reflect its importance for their marital bond with its neatness and well tended, serene atmosphere. Often, the baby's cradle is in there as well, and it should be given a spot that ensures that baby's things aren't strewn around but have their own place, even though baby's time there is short.

Often, we find that the nuptial bedroom gets the least attention of all the rooms, but the couple should not fall prey to this temptation, for the sake of the family's happiness, which depends on the marital bond for its foundation.

The parents' room might have a crucifix over the head of the bed. An image of our Lady, a bottle of holy water, and a prie-dieu might be nice additions.

Children's rooms

Contrary to popular belief, children thrive when they share bedrooms. It's not necessary or even advisable for young children to be alone in rooms, if possible. As they get older, a girls' room and a boys' room is often enough to accommodate even a large family. Children love multiple bunk beds in a room. The idea for separate rooms for children came about with the habit of sending children to their rooms for their waking activities. But it's better for child development if children use their rooms for sleeping, spending their waking hours in the common rooms of the house. Making quiet time a part of every day ensures that work and prayer can take place, even in the common space.

Since bedrooms are to be primarily for sleeping, keep the toys in the family areas. Children who grow up entertaining their guests in the family rooms and using their electronic equipment under Mother's watchful eye are less likely later on to develop problems that we in America associate with teenagers.

If possible, place beds opposite the door and pulled out from the wall so that each side can be accessed. That way, making the bed is easier. Usually bedrooms have ceiling lights, but it's really desirable to have bedside lamps as well—they can be clipped on the frame itself or be on a bedside table. On a dresser top or bedside table, there might be a small statue or icon, a vial of holy water, and a crucifix (which could also be above the bed or across from the bed on the opposite wall, to be the first object seen upon waking).

Low, long dressers are best for children's clothes and personal items to be accessible, and shelving or a hutch can safely keep special mementoes from being broken by curious little ones' hands.

Living area

We dare make the bold observation that most living spaces in our culture today are oriented to the television. We'd like to give you another way of thinking of things.

The living area can be carefully thought out so that family members and guests can sit in comfort to visit and enjoy each other's conversation. It's nice to consider the possibility of playing games (other than video games) together and joining in singing and playing instruments.

However, since in family life, the shared entertainment is often watching sports or movies together, it's reasonable to consider comfort for viewing the screen. Certainly, viewing something as a family at home is preferable (and not only economically) to going out very often! But it should be possible and indeed easy to have a conversation without reference to the TV. A large-screen TV is a dominant presence in the room. If the TV can be covered when not in use, so much the better.

Another idea is to place an ottoman or a low-cushioned bench in front of the TV so that, when it's off, a couple of children or other hardy souls can sit facing the others. It is also nice to have more than just one solitary sofa, so that the people aren't forced to sit in a row and face the same direction—that is, toward the TV.

The furniture should be welcoming, clean, and organized in a semicircle so that people can see each other without straining. (The single most frequently committed mistake in homes is to arrange seating too far apart for easy conversation and eye contact.) Extra seating is always welcome in the form of floor cushions and a soft carpet. Throw pillows and afghans on the seating to help complete the coziness.

There should be good lighting, with lamps providing warm pools of light so people can read without strain and to relieve harsh shadows from overhead fixtures. Pictures, photos, and mementoes that are particular to the family should be displayed at the eye level of a rather short person—most people put their decorations up too high. Grouping displays adds interest.

When folks gather to pray in the living area, there might be a place that is natural to put a lighted candle: a mantel or some sort of credenza or coffee table. On the wall, among the artwork and the family photos, there might be a crucifix and a Marian icon or a painting to remind us of our Faith.

Kitchen
The kitchen's storage will be greatly enhanced by plate racks and hutches for storage. Usually the sink faces a window and a view, if the cook—or at least the person who washes the dishes—is lucky. Sometimes there is a counter that opens to another room; sometimes there is a wall.

Whatever the view, the woman of the house arranges the area above the sink to display pretty things she loves: a picture of our Lady, a vase for a flower, a pot of herbs for quick access to liven a dish, a handmade item from a child. It's very important that this area not be allowed to collect debris (rubber bands, which could be put in a container in a drawer; broken pieces of things, which should probably be discarded; stray parts of toys, which should be put on the kitchen table for attention from their owners, etc.). The person who does the dishes should have something lovely and contemplative to look at!

Eating areas

In the dining room (or the eating area in the kitchen), the table setting often reflects the changing season, liturgical and natural, with a wreath, a vase of flowers, or a bowl of decorated eggs (if you blow out the contents of the eggs, they last forever — or until broken!). The mantel or sideboard can be a place to display a religious object and a votive candle.

Other places

A home often has other areas — hallways, entrances, a porch, a mudroom, a pantry, and so forth. Each place has its own function and orderliness appropriate thereto — and don't underestimate the value of shelves in each of them. A back hall can be brightly painted and tidy. Even the mudroom can be painted a bright, light color to be welcoming and exude an air of orderly purposefulness.

The hallway to the bedrooms can have a holy-water font so that everyone can bless himself before bed.

A door to the exterior of the house can have a small mirror so that guests and family members can check their appearance before leaving.

A religious image that one sees as he enters or leaves the house is referred to sometimes as "the doorkeeper." We can teach the children (and ourselves) to glance at this image with a little prayer.

THE LITTLE ORATORY IN THE HOME

"A little oratory of this kind, though it may remain hidden from the eyes of men, is what turns a dwelling of any Christian into a 'domestic church'! Like a pinch of salt, which seems to disappear in the world, it actually flavours and seasons it" (Fr. Gabriel Byrne, *Earthen Vessels*).

Where does the little oratory fit into the setting up of the home? Where and how do we pray as a family?

The *Catechism* recommends that we consider appropriate places for personal prayer: "For personal prayer, this can be a 'prayer corner' with the Sacred Scriptures

and icons, in order to be there, in secret, before our Father. In a Christian family, this kind of little oratory fosters prayer in common" (CCC 2691).

PLACING THE HOME ALTAR

The home has a natural flow of movement—people come and go and frequent certain spots more than others. It's sometimes suggested to make a prayer closet or separate room, and some people really need that for their own personal prayer. The Gospel of Matthew tells us, "But thou when thou shalt pray, enter into thy chamber, and having shut the door, pray to thy Father in secret: and thy Father who seeth in secret will repay thee" (Matt. 6:6, Douay-Rheims). Of course, this can be interpreted literally or figuratively: the "chamber" can be an actual one or the chamber of the heart, the interior castle. The point, very often overlooked, is that the soul must have some time alone with God in a completely interior, intimate way.

We've used some words interchangeably—prayer table, home altar, icon corner. The idea, especially, of an icon *corner* can suggest an out-of-the-way place. But for family prayer, it's better for the home altar or even the icon corner to be somewhere where the family daily passes by or rests, so that it isn't forgotten.

So think about the flow in your own home. Is there a place that seems fittingly out in the open, but not too quickly breezed by? (For instance, a front hallway might have a good spot for a side table that could be easily made into a prayer table, but the fact that it's where people are on their way in or out ultimately might make it unsuitable.)

Very often a corner or interior wall in the dining room or the living room will be just right. Stand where you enter the room, and see where your eyes naturally land. That may be a good place to put an image of the face of Christ, which is the anchor of prayer, and then the little oratory will take shape from there.

Ideally, the placement of the home altar should be so that the person praying is facing east. Praying toward the east expresses our expectation of the coming of the Son, symbolized by the rising sun. Churches are traditionally oriented toward, well, the orient! That is to say, the east. This may be a consideration only if you can design and build your own home!

You are looking for a place that is just right for a corner shelf or a small side table or even for a hutch that just calls out to be the focal point of your family's prayer life. And it might not be confined to one place, depending on the size of your house, although a friend with a quite small house has both a corner and a small table very near each other. It works quite naturally.

It's possible, especially in a very small house or an apartment, to have the focal point for devotions be something other than a table or a corner. A natural spot (even arising etymologically from the word *focal*, which means "of the hearth") would be the mantel. So often the mantel is treated as one more horizontal surface to clutter, but it can be cleared off and lovingly arranged with sacred objects (or just beautiful objects that the family enjoys looking at). In the past few decades, a reaction against a stuffily decorated mantel has resulted in an aesthetic that discards symmetry, but the prayer place must have symmetry (but doesn't need to be stuffy!). We will go further into this idea of how to arrange things in the next chapter. Thought and care can make the mantel a very good place for prayer gathering.

Another natural spot is the main eating table—the kitchen table if that is the only one, or the dining table if the family gathers there for the evening meal. A pretty tray or a shallow wooden box set up in the center and holding the appropriate elements can very well be the focal point for the family's prayer.

A third spot that comes to mind is the sideboard in the dining room. Often a hutch or a dresser can be arranged to be the physical place where the family turns for prayer.

Finding the right location might take time and experimentation. Try something and see how it works. Very often, actual use will suggest the place; so don't be discouraged if the first attempt has to be changed. That's not a sign of defeat at all, but of learning!

Once you've chosen a fitting place for your home altar, you can think about what goes on and above (and even under) it, and this is what we will discuss in the next chapter.

Making the Little Oratory in the Home

Even the sparrow finds a home,
and the swallow a nest for herself,
where she may lay her young,
at your altars, O Lord of hosts,
my King and my God.

Psalm 84:3

In this chapter we get to the details of making your little oratory. Perhaps you already have the idea and are ready to go. Wonderful! Or perhaps you might not have a mental image or any experience with creating something like this and want your hand held. That's what we are here for.

The idea is that you love the thought of having a little oratory and will make it your very own.

Here is the advantage, besides all the lofty thoughts of the previous two chapters: at last, a place for those things that float around your house — the odd statue, the prayer cards, the icons, the rosaries. Gathering them into one place, you will find that they become more than the sum of their parts. They no longer are just things to look at (or, worse, to attract dust while we don't look at them); they become a shrine.

The word *shrine* may conjure only a neglected corner; something that was thought of once but later abandoned. Or a shrine may suggest to you an impression made while speeding along the highway — of favorite sneakers, teddy bears, and a plastic wreath by a roadside cross. Yet even that image bespeaks a longing to reach something beyond, however clumsily executed.

The shrine we speak of is meant to be simply a place of beauty, directing our gaze through carefully chosen representative objects toward the transcendent.

IT WILL BE HOLY AND LOVELY

Some readers will intuitively know how to make this place in their home. I suspect these are the same folks who are good at arranging furniture, choosing paint colors, keeping their floors swept, and in general, having a knack for order (*order* here meaning not only tidiness but also a sense of what is fitting overall). In the homes of such folks, even a humble object seems like more than itself. Even the way they arrange their dishes or pillows seems intentional and definitely conveys confidence. Something of value is being communicated, even with inanimate objects.

The rest of us like to have a detailed discussion of all the elements, and that is what we will provide here, with an emphasis on detail — with some theory thrown in as well, to keep things connected to our goals.

We promise to keep in mind that you may very well have a population of wild youngsters underfoot, and possibly a semidomesticated pet or two. We will also keep in mind that you may very well not have a big budget — which will be easy enough to do, because neither do we.

Your part is to keep in mind that you have complete freedom of expression. Make your little oratory communicate your own faith in our Lord, without slavish dependency on what any perceived authority might seem to dictate. It's true that tradition — in many cases, alas, lost by now — can offer us a framework. It's always good to see what those who lived the Faith in a strong environment have done, and it would be foolish to neglect what that collective memory has to offer us.

On the other hand, the neglect brought on by the passage of time can obscure beauty, and your very own fresh approach may be just what is needed. So please take all these suggestions as being offered with the utmost respect for the genius of the household — your family's own creativity.

THE TABLE OR SHELF

In this section, we discuss setting up the table and covering it.

If your home altar isn't in an actual corner (discussed below), you will probably need a table (and what is said here can be applied to a sideboard, a mantel, or another horizontal surface, as touched upon in the previous chapter). The size and height of this table will be determined by the space, of course, but you will probably have good luck finding something that is about waist high and about eighteen inches deep — and two and a half or three feet across seems to be a good width. The type of side table called a console or sofa table works very well, as it is the right height and isn't too deep.

It's important to have something that is high enough to be out of reach of a grabby toddler, but not so high that an interested child can't see; perhaps this makes a table preferable to a corner shelf.

If you check the dimensions of the area where you are interested in putting the table, you will be able to recognize a table that will fit there when you see one. Keep an eye out for a table at garage and yard sales and thrift shops. Since you are going to be fixing it up and covering its top with a cloth, it doesn't have to be in wonderful condition.

And what if the table you find is, in fact, in a somewhat battered state? There are many ways to rescue furniture, so don't pass the piece over if it is the right size. Here are some thoughts:

You want the legs of the table to be solid and in a style you like. Inspect the way it's constructed. Often just a tightening of screws can fix the wobbles.

If the finish is good, lucky you! If not, and the legs are metal, you can sand any rust off, wipe them well to remove all the dust, and paint them with metallic spray paint. If the legs are made of good wood, such as walnut or cherry, you can sand them and apply a new finish. You can get all sorts of easily applied polyurethanes, but beeswax polish[2] is a favorite, because it gives a deep luster to wood, even if you're dealing with something that is not of great quality.

If the legs are made of wood that is of inferior quality, you can paint them (spray paint is durable and easy to apply, but any enamel paint will work).

If the top is banged up, you can sand it down and apply beeswax, as with the legs (and it's fine to have painted legs and a poly'd or beeswaxed top). Don't worry about staining it if that seems daunting, because you will likely

---

[2] Mix four parts mineral oil to one part beeswax by volume, melted together in a jar in a double boiler. When you want to use it, heat it gently in the double boiler or microwave and use a clean cloth to rub it on. Then buff it with a soft, dry cloth.

have a cloth over it (see next page). If it's laminate, you might want to paint over it with a special paint for that purpose.

Even if the table isn't of an ideal size, you can get started with what you find and upgrade later. Start with something, even if it seems too small, even if you can only find a bookcase or a sideboard or even a crate. Just start.

A SHELF

The Eastern way, sometimes also seen in the West but not as frequently, is to have a prayer corner shelf. You have two options: you can install a shelf in the corner, or you can find a corner hutch.

If the objects that assist your devotion are mainly icons (or Western images—of the Sacred Heart and the Immaculate Heart of Mary, for instance), displaying them in a corner is ideal, rather than having them spread out on one wall, although that can be done as well, so remain flexible.

Your challenge will be to place the shelf at the right height, perhaps a little lower than you think, so that children can see it. You might want to have a little sturdy stepstool that can be pulled out and stood on. The stool can be painted to fit in, even if it does double duty in the room.

There are several ways to get a shelf up in a corner. Any way you do it, be sure to locate the studs in the wall where you want it to go. If you

have small, decorative brackets, you can install those and rest your shelf on them, with another support at the apex of the board (which will be hidden by it once it's installed). You can also screw supporting strips of wood into the studs. The wood strips should be about half an inch by half an inch and the length of your shelf, minus two or three inches, so that you won't see them when everything is in place. One strip should be half an inch shorter than the other, so that the longer one can go right into the corner and the shorter one can abut it.

Once those strips are installed, you can screw your shelf onto them, creating a sturdy surface strong enough to support a few religious items. The shelf can be purchased prefinished at a home-improvement store (and they do carry nice ones with the edge that faces the room being curved outward), or you can make one from a piece of wood that is half an inch thick (or the thickness that appeals to you), cutting it at a 45-degree angle across. You might want to check the squareness of your corner, as some corners aren't all they should be in the right-angle department. If necessary, you can clip off the point of your shelf to avoid odd fitting problems.

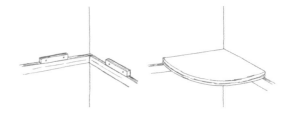

In thrift stores you can find appealing corner shelves that will work very well in your icon corner or serve as inspiration for making your own. It's well worth looking at images of shelves to see the variety and creativity. Shelves truly help make a house a home! You may find that once you organize your icon corner, you will be inspired to apply the same idea to other areas in your house.

A CLOTH FOR YOUR PRAYER TABLE

On the altar in church, the cloth is a sign of respect for the sacred object, and the altar itself is a representation of the sacrifice, that is, Christ (1 Pet. 2:4), as well as "that which sanctifies the offering" (cf. Matt 23:19). Certainly, the cloth in church not only provides protection for the altar but also adds beauty and mystery.

In the home, the cloth enhances the prayer corner. A cloth can really make the difference in how the little oratory looks. When you are thinking that things look a little spare and a little lacking in cohesion, try a cloth—or even a bit of lace—to see how things come together.

In the next chapters, we will discuss how the home altar helps us live the liturgical year of the Church. You have probably noticed, in church, that the liturgical season is indicated by the color of the clerical vestments. You can use different colored cloths at the table at home as well: dark green for ordinary time; violet for Lent and Advent; white for Easter; red for the time of the Passion, between Palm Sunday and Good Friday, and for Pentecost.

Fibers and sizes

We recommend natural fibers only. Linen is the textile that stays looking crisp and rewards care the most. Starch and iron a piece of linen, and just appreciate how handsome it is!

Cotton works well. Fine wool and silk are lovely, but not as easy to care for. And it's up to you how simple—even a piece of burlap could work—or fancy—such as a treasured bit of lace from long ago—you want the table to be. Handmade—homespun, hand woven, hand tatted, hand embroidered—is always preferable to machine made, although the latter can have its own beauty as well.

If you have a particular ethnic heritage and own a colorful textile that represents your background, why not use it here? Maybe your grandmother's linens came down to you and you haven't found a good use for them. Some of those large dinner napkins are too fussy for the dining room but would be perfect on your prayer table. Maybe someone brought you a textile from a trip abroad and you haven't figured out yet what to do with it. Think of your home altar.

The best cloth for the home altar doesn't hang down in front or too much on the sides, for staying out of temptation's way. Little children can wreak too much havoc in too short a time for dangling fabric to work! But a table runner is ideal. For the small corner shelf, a lace doily fits perfectly. For the prayer table, a prayer shawl might be just right.

Laundering

Sometimes thrifted linens are soiled and stained. Here is what you can do to try to rescue them. Inspect their condition. If they seem sturdy and are white or unbleached, treat any spots with an oxygen-type stain remover and lukewarm water. Rub a little detergent into the stain, and rinse well.

For oil stains, you need a heavy-duty grease-stain remover. In some areas of the country you can buy Lestoil, a great grease remover; otherwise look for a product that contains aromatic mineral spirits, called Stoddard solvent. Put a little on the stain, rub in gently, let it sit for twenty minutes, and then wash the cloth in warm water with your regular detergent.

If the stains remain and the item is 100 percent cotton, wash it in warm water and a quarter cup of chlorine bleach per small load of water. If it's linen, use cold water. After the bleach is well mixed with the water, let the cloth soak for at least twenty minutes. Then run the cycle on permanent press or delicate — it's the heat and the bleach that will get the stains out, not the agitation of the machine, which might rip apart delicate work.

If a bit of lace or embroidery seems almost hopelessly stained, and you've tried the gentle, cautious methods, try hotter water and whatever stain-removal method you can. You have nothing to lose.

Dry the cloth in the sunshine, which works wonders where chemicals fail. Spread a clean sheet on the lawn and lay the cloth on it for as long as there is full sun. In any case, use the dryer only on the low/delicate setting if at all. Even hanging the cloth on a rack indoors is less wearing on fabric than the dryer.

If there is candle wax on the cloth, scrape away as much of it as you can with a butter knife, and then run hot tap water over the wax, through the fabric, until it melts away.

If your cloth is silk or wool, you can wash it in lukewarm water and a gentle liquid detergent meant for hand washables. Treat these delicate fibers with a light touch. Spread the cloth on a rack to dry.

Iron your cloth: For cotton or linen, use your highest setting and steam. Spray starch will take a drab wrinkled mess into a respectable to honored state. For silk, use a medium/low setting (start on the lower end and gradually increase the heat to the level that just gets the wrinkles out). Make sure your steam is off, because silk can easily get water stains.

Our foremothers always used a pressing cloth made of cotton or linen, like an old but very clean dishtowel, dampened well, between the wool and the iron to avoid burning the fibers.

A high steam setting and medium/high heat works fine without that press cloth, but again, proceed with caution. Test the setting on an inconspicuous corner of the wrong side of the piece.

Remember that you are going to be placing objects on your cloth, and you can do so strategically to cover stains and little holes! Sometimes a beautiful old piece is worth a little sleight of hand to make it work.

IMAGES

And what should go on and around and above a prayer table?

To get you started, we offer here a detailed discussion of the images you might include in the little oratory, how to discern their beauty, and how to place them. After which, you will find an explicated list of the other elements that go on and around the prayer table.

The arrangement of the images

Imprint Christ ... onto your heart, where he [already] dwells; whether you read a book about him, or behold him in an image, may he inspire your thoughts, as you come to know him twofold through the twofold experience of your senses. Thus you will see with your eyes what you have learned through the words you have heard. He who in this way hears

and sees will fill his entire being with the praise of God.[3]

It might be helpful to see what tradition has to tell us in the arrangement of images. In the Byzantine icon-corner tradition, the order has been preserved, and that can be very instructive to those of us who are trying to figure things out from scratch, as there is much wisdom in these ancient ways.

The center and the crux, so to speak, of our Faith, is Christ suffering on the Cross—the Crucifixion, the living God, offering Himself as a perfect sacrifice for our sakes.

Thus, centerpiece of the little oratory is the crucifix: that is to say, a cross with a corpus on it, not an empty or bare cross. A freestanding crucifix on a base will anchor everything on a corner shelf and will work on a table as well, as will a wall crucifix centered above the table.

To the right of the crucifix should be a picture of Christ glorified, such as a traditional icon of Christ in majesty, a picture of the Transfiguration, a painting of the Sacred Heart of Jesus, or one of the face of Christ on a cloth (a Veronica cloth image would be a Western version; the Mandylion is the Eastern version).

To the left of the crucifix should be an image of our Lady, the Mother of God.

---

[3] Theodore the Studite against the heresy of iconoclasm, ninth century; quoted in Christoph Schönborn, *God's Human Face* (San Francisco: Ignatius Press, 1994), 232.

These three images, Christ suffering on the Cross, Christ glorified, and the Mother of God, are the beating heart of every prayer corner. If you can find a crucifix, all you will need for your own little oratory is to pull out the color prints in this book that appeal to you, frame them attractively, and hang them. Your home altar will be ready to go.

What is it about an image that helps prayer?
Sometimes it seems as if people use religious art, even in churches but also in their homes, as an element of the décor. They don't seem to be directly engaging with it at all. Often, if we observe them in church, we notice that people don't really look at the art (for instance, a statue of our Lady), but often pray with their eyes shut.

Religious art can be a great help for the spiritual life if we consider how to interact with it. It's not a matter of staring at it, trying to experience it in a way that whips up the emotions. Some guides we've read recommend something along these lines, which seems overly elaborate and pseudo-mystical, not conveying any real meaning.

Let's look at a traditional way of using religious art in prayer. At the prayer table, we can begin facing the image that fits with our prayer. If we are invoking the intercession of a saint, we can look at the image of the saint. If we are praying the Our Father, we can look at the crucifix or the image of Christ.

Pray as you usually do, but look at the picture or statue just as you would a photo of your spouse. It's a reminder. In art, however, every aspect of the work is (or should be) chosen to engage us in the dynamic of prayer, directing our hearts and minds to heaven. The symbols, the backgrounds, the colors—everything directs our gaze beyond itself to the reality it depicts. All of this enhances our efforts to speak to the person, whether it is God, whom we are worshipping, or a saint we are invoking or honoring.

The style of the image

It is not just an image's content (*what* is painted) that is important, but also its style (*how* it is painted). Aside from influencing our taste and developing our sense of the beautiful, the images we look at while we pray will also be the seed ground of our imagination, influencing what appears in our mind's eye (and especially when we pray with our eyes closed). The style is the manifestation of the beauty; it catches our attention. So it is important that we pick good art.

Just as the Eucharist, celebrated in the Liturgy, is the source and summit of Christian life (CCC 1324), so liturgical art is the source of inspiration for all other art and the summit to which all other art directs us. If that art is good, it will affect the culture for the good; if it is bad, the reverse is true. Art is very important.

It's notoriously difficult and dangerous to give advice on taste, however. We would not venture to try. Although what is traditional has stood the test of time, by definition, there is room for a personal response to art, for local traditions, and for the possibility of developing new styles. At the same time, we ought to have standards for what is appropriate in religious art specifically and avoid the ugly, the superficial, the merely sentimental, and the downright kitschy.

Perhaps we can help by asking good questions about art, perhaps, without setting up an Inquisition on Beauty. Some questions might be the following:

• *Is it beautiful?* It's surprising how often people are uncomfortable applying this standard, seemingly so obvious, to religious art. Perhaps they feel they might hurt God's feelings by rejecting a picture of Christ or a saint that is simply ugly. Feel free to reject such art.

• *Does it reflect the truth?* Is the content of the image consistent with the teachings of the Church? For example, a picture of the Creation we have seen that shows many human forms emerging from a swirling disorder is not consistent with the teaching of the Church that we are all descended from one couple, Adam and Eve. Thus, while it may be beautiful in style, it is not fitting in content.

• *Would I spend eternity (or at least a long time) with this?* Usually what we put in the little oratory will stay there permanently. Let it be of lasting quality.

• *Is it well done?* As with ugly religious art, sometimes poorly done art is hard for us to reject because we like to be nice. But it's valid to ask if the style is well done when we compare it with other sacred art, which we will discuss later. And the materials should be excellent, including the presentation (for example, a good frame).

The main thing is to choose beautiful images with suitable content that nourish your prayer. We've provided images in this book that conform in content and execution to the venerable traditions of the Church. We hope that you find them beautiful enough to use in your home.

It doesn't have to be an icon

The traditions of the Church are good guides. Some people today suggest that only iconographic images, such as we might see in a Greek or Russian Orthodox Church, are appropriate for sacred art — that the icon form is in some way inherently superior to other Catholic traditions in art. This is not so. While the icon is good, it is not the only style that tradition has to offer.

Iconography developed in the first centuries of the Church. All the variations conform (often in different ways) to a style developed to communicate visually a sense of mankind in heaven, of the already sanctified person.

Icons have an abstraction that can seem odd to those whose idea of art is that it should depict the world in a naturalistic way. Icons are more symbolic than those schooled in Western art are accustomed to. For instance, the reason that saints in icons are shown either full or three-quarter face is so that both eyes will be visible to the viewer. This is symbolic of

perfect purity and clarity — there is no secret, dark side to the person. A person depicted in profile in an icon is one who has rejected God definitively. Every feature of an icon has some symbolic intent.

Other fitting traditions

In the West, art forms became more naturalistic and less abstract in style after the original iconographic period. The change reflected a desire to show man on his *way* to heaven, that is, on his pilgrimage here on earth. The styles of art that best combine beauty and theological significance, according to Pope Benedict XVI in *The Spirit of the Liturgy*, are the Gothic and the Baroque "at its best." In these styles, symbols, although still important, give way to personal expression and an emphasis on the natural, earthly qualities of man's existence. In particular, the most striking difference is in the use of light and shadow, expressive of a stylistic vocabulary that explores the meaning of sin and evil in the world, as well as God's grace and redemption. The content, however, is still any scene appropriate for sacred art.

Later styles and schools of art may still offer objects of beauty. However, by the nineteenth century, art became an exercise in the rejection of tradition and Christianity and an exaltation of the individual, divorced from his relationship to God. As a result, from this point on, there is no coherent artistic tradition that is authentically liturgical — that is to say, expressive of the communion of man and God that arises from the Incarnation and is consummated in the Passion.

In the mid-twentieth century, a number of Russians living in Paris, and some Greeks who had contact with them, did a lot of work to reestablish the tradition that had all but died out in the thirteenth century. They carefully discerned the essence of iconography and laid out principles to guide patrons and painters. Through their work, the tradition of iconography was reestablished. It was because of their nationality that so many people think, incorrectly, that the icon form is exclusively Russian or Greek.

Training one's eye by looking at art from the styles mentioned here—the icon form, the Gothic style, and the Baroque style—helps in evaluating something in another style or from another artistic tradition. And not every authentic expression will be formal or grand. For instance, some religious art of very high quality is done in a folk or even primitive style (think of the images reproduced in the *Catechism of the Catholic Church* that come from the catacombs and are luminous in their simplicity). The idea is that not only the content, but also the style itself is integrated with the values of the Liturgy: through our senses we are taken up to the realm of the spirit.

Still, in any age there are artists who are inspired in their work, despite any faults in their training. The art of our time ought to participate in the timeless principles of beauty, taking the good of the past and presenting it in a new yet connected form, in tandem with the liturgical renewal (which itself is nourished by tradition). Then the art forms produced for churches can once again engender other forms of culture by their beauty.

For your home, avoid anything contrived or distorted, or somehow rejecting tradition, even if it is an innovative work. Choose images that relate to Tradition and the Liturgy in a beautiful way. It may very well be possible to find (or make!) new art that does this.

OTHER OBJECTS FOR THE PRAYER TABLE

Candles

A word about perceived fire danger: There are some today who are completely anti-candle. Of course, we've all heard terrible stories of whole houses—and even lives—being lost due to fires started by candles.

A lit candle that tips over in your presence can simply be extinguished. The danger is when you leave the room or the house while candles are burning and there are flammable objects nearby. Of course, for centuries, banks of candles have burned away in churches—set in iron stands in stone grottos. Nothing to catch fire there!

Do you know that the *votive* in *votive candles* means "for prayer"? They are safer than candlesticks, nicely settled in their glass holders. Candles really meant for church use are balanced in size, shape, and quality so that they really burn, all the way to the bottom (candles made for decoration, even when they are more expensive, don't always burn properly). You can light these and leave them burning without worrying that something will catch fire (although please don't leave one lit through the night or when going out).

So use your common sense. We would be loath to lose the mystery and wonder provided by candlelight!

Candlelight has the effect of drawing the spirit toward itself. It's soft and heartening. Its pure light can't help but remind us of its source, the sun, and beyond the sun to the source of creation, Jesus, the Light of the World.

Candles bring a warmth and a purifying scent into the room in which they're used. Just simply have candles on the table and in front of a holy picture or statue and *light them*!

A votive candle is definitely the safest choice for the little oratory. Sometimes when we're gathered for a special prayer around our mantel, we light tapers in candlesticks. Certainly, in church this is what is done.

A word on symmetry

Somehow, in universally electrified twentieth-century America, candles became decorative only. They weren't lit. They were just put there. And then something truly disturbing crept into decorating styles and crawled over into liturgical use.

I speak of the choice to put two candlesticks on one side of a mantel, say, with something—for instance, a vase or a stack of books—balancing it on the other side. In the church, on the altar, this became simply candles on one side and flowers on the other.

But surely you see what a poor decision this is. It's entirely predicated on the assumption that the candles will not be lit—that they are simply objects with no function. If their function—to illuminate—is taken into consideration for even an instant, it becomes clear that they must be placed symmetrically. To do otherwise is to destroy their raison d'être, to go against what gives them beauty as objects in the first place, namely, their ability to provide light. If they are not on the table to provide light, first and foremost, they shouldn't be there at all, as we don't want *things* there—we want beautiful things that *serve* our devotion.

Symmetry as a design element can be argued and left up to individual taste for the most part. Balance and symmetry are part of a pleasing arrangement, but there is no need for a rigid duplication of the space—we don't promote the idea that whatever appears on one side must be repeated on the other. In this book we try to emphasize freedom and a lively application of whatever suits you in these matters. But please, if you have two candles, put them on either side of your prayer space.

Censers

In the Eastern tradition, a censer, something that seems optional in the Western home, is a fixture. The idea of incense is a lovely one. Psalm 141:2, expresses the meaning of the sweet-smelling smoke that rises upward like a supplication:

> *Let my prayer be counted*
> *as incense before thee,*
> *and the lifting up of my hands*
> *as an evening sacrifice!*

A thurible, or censer (the two names are for the same object: a metal container for burning incense), can be hung on a hook attached to the wall. There are also little censers that sit on a fireproof saucer. Censers are easily lit using a small piece of charcoal and a few grains of incense.

Incense can be purchased at stores that sell church goods or at various sites online — maybe even from your parish church, because you don't need much. Here (as with candles, by the way), you will have to navigate "magical" waters and avoid treading a path to the occult, which movement has somewhat taken over the incense-and-candle trade. Let's reclaim it for pure purposes, being careful to guard our eyes as we shop.

You can light your incense when you pray, and even after the charcoal goes out, the fragrance remains. It's another reminder of the sanctification of our senses and the general approval with which our Faith regards the created world. We use beautiful-smelling things not to escape this world but to bring this world into the next.

The use of incense in the Liturgy is bound with very precise rules, down to the number of swings of the thurible. At home, you have complete freedom to do what seems fitting.

A place for matches and spent matches

You can take any attractive small box and glue a bit of striking plate from a box of matches on the inside cover or the underside. Then store your matches in the box. That way, you won't need to have unsightly matchbooks or matchboxes lying around.

Have a small metal or porcelain dish or brass pot for placing spent matches in. Never throw a used match in the wastebasket. One, at least, of your authors has started a fire this way! A match has to be quite cold for a while to be ready to be thrown in the bin. (Of course, you can briefly douse it with water, but this would require walking from your prayer corner to the sink, which is why we suggest a little container for the spent matches, to be emptied later, perhaps by a dutiful child.)

Easel or stand

A small tabletop easel or stand can really help with flat icons or images that you would like to display upright and change

with the season or feast day. Keep your eye open for such things in secondhand shops. Anything can work. Avoid anything showy that suggests contemporary decorating trends. But anything simple or ornate in a traditional or artistic vein would be lovely.

Bible

We aren't recommending keeping a Bible *only* on the prayer table. Bibles in every room get used. We need them in bedrooms for private devotions, and the big family Bible might be kept in the living room. But if your prayer table is large enough, you might want to keep a Bible there, on a bookstand or flat on the table, or on a shelf underneath if the surface area isn't large enough. It's worthwhile to have a special place to keep the children's Bibles, so that they won't get thrown around or treated like any common children's book.

Prayer books

Prayer books will be useful for your prayer table. Here are some books to think about acquiring:

• *Breviary.* We will discuss the Liturgy of the Hours at length in chapter 5. You can keep your family Breviary (or Breviaries) on a shelf under or near the prayer table.

• *Rosary books.* It's nice to have pictures of the Mysteries of the Rosary that children can look at while praying the Rosary. Choose books with simple, classic line drawings or artwork from

beautiful sources — for the sake of longevity, it's better to avoid childish cartoons.

• *Books of blessings and compendia of devotions,* especially the Stations of the Cross to be used during Lent.

Prayer-intention journal

A beautiful journal, which serves as a prayer-intention book, can be on the prayer table or underneath on a shelf. Not every prayer intention has to go in there, but when someone asks for prayers, or when a very important intention comes up, it's wonderful to write it down. Note the date and whatever information you can. Later, on reading the intentions, you will find that God answered the prayers in ways foreseen and unforeseen. It's not a bad idea to have a dedicated pen nearby.

Vases

Flowers are an important part of how we show love and affection to God and the saints. Little children know this. If they can get to anything growing, they will delightedly pull it out of the ground and bring it to you, with burning love.

Wise parents channel this incorrigible tendency. With gentle instructions as to what can and cannot be picked and low expectations as to immediate results in following these instructions, parents will keep a few vases in a low cupboard or on the shelf below the little oratory. A child can get the vase himself, arrange the flowers, add a little water from a small pitcher also stored there, and place it near the crucifix or a statue of our Lady.

As the children get a bit older (but even a three-year-old can learn this), teach them to strip the lower leaves off the part of the stem that will be in the water, to keep the water fresher. Show them how to wipe up spills (after all, it's just water). Send them to discard spent blooms and clean the vessels.

May is a good time to focus on this activity. Traditionally, the May altar blooms for our Lady, no doubt the resort of the resigned mother who knows that her children *will* bring in the first buds, no matter what she says! But what better destiny for the flowers? Every image can have its little vase with even one bud to show our love for the Blessed Mother.

In winter, branches can be used. In late winter, buds of flowering trees are easily forced —simply cut them with sharp shears and place the branches in water. Soon the buds will appear. Pussy willows dry nicely, so don't put them in water—they will keep the altar pretty until spring arrives for real.

Blessed palms can be placed here until they are ready to be burned.

Prayer cards

Ever wonder what to do with the prayer cards you collect, commemorating the children's patron saints, special prayers, our Lady, and funerals? They proliferate.

The prayer table is the answer. You can keep the cards in a little box, decorated appropriately; a cigar box works well, covered in pretty paper, or a wooden box with paint, or a vintage tin. You will find that a child will ask to have the box down so that he can sort through the cards, which he will do quietly and with great devotion. Special ones can be rotated through and displayed on a little easel on feast days. Cards picturing patron saints can be kept out as a fixture of the table, of course.

In November, the funeral memorial cards can be set out as a reminder to pray for the dearly departed. (See chapter 6 for a detailed discussion of devotions tied to certain months, including our prayers for the faithful departed.)

Objects on the wall other than paintings
Besides paintings and icons that can be hung on the wall, you might want a decorative hook or rack for rosaries, and one for your censer if it's the kind that hangs on a chain. A plant hanger would work very well—something that comes out from the wall about six inches.

Anything on the wall should relate to the other things—be close to them and not too high up. Most people make the mistake of hanging things too high. And when children are to be included, lower is better anyway. Things look best when they are grouped with like things or with symmetry or balance.

Kneeler

Some people like to have a kneeler or prie-dieu in front of or next to the home altar. When the parents use the kneeler for their own personal prayer during the day, the children naturally fall into the habit of using it themselves. At first they seem simply to kneel there, but eventually, after a few questions or simple conversations, they learn to pray interiorly themselves.

CARE OF THE TABLE AND ITS OBJECTS

A lot of people don't understand what dusting is, as funny as that seems; they may have the idea that dusting is the vague flicking of particles into the air with a feather duster, and consequently their decorating, holy and otherwise, suffers. If instead you think of dusting as *wiping the object down*, you will get somewhere.

The table itself needs to be wiped down occasionally. Substances in the air cling to the furniture due to moisture and ionization. If you get a damp cloth (dampened either with water or an inert cleaning oil—don't use vegetable oil, which becomes rancid and gummy) and rub it down, it will be freshened up. Start by removing every single thing on the table or shelf. Wipe the surface and the legs. Then replace the things one by one if they really belong there (horizontal surfaces, however holy, do seem to attract all sorts of random things!).

Clean the prayer-table cloth as outlined earlier. Or at least give it a shake.

Wipe each object as you replace it. Metal things can be cleaned and polished according to their substances—tarnish removed and wax melted with hot water or flaked off after freezing. Vases should be emptied and washed with soapy water. Statues and frames can be wiped.

A feather duster or microfiber duster can actually be helpful to restore a bit of sparkle and shine to the table quickly without moving anything, but it's not a substitute for the occasional real wiping down of everything with a damp cloth.

We always find that things in general accumulate—even things that are supposed to be there—because there are too many. If this is the case, decide how to rotate the objects. Put the ones you are not using on a shelf beneath the prayer table or in a box or a drawer.

BEAUTY

After such a long discussion of practical matters, we'd like to turn again to beauty, the quality that we most wish to express in making our little oratory, whether it is simple or grand.

In Psalm 19, the psalmist expresses his joy in looking upward: "The heavens proclaim the glory of the Lord" (cf. Ps. 19:1). In just the same way, if our places of worship are beautiful, then they too will proclaim the glory of the Lord, just by virtue of their beauty.

These are some ideas for establishing your own little oratory. Above all, regardless of its simplicity or otherwise, make it beautiful. Its beauty will convey more of faith than anything else. For most of us, this beauty really will be expressed in simplicity. Although we have

carefully tried to go over any and all the things that could be included, we want to be sure that you understand that we aren't recommending necessarily having them all. Some homes are grand enough to have a chapel! Some will have only a small shelf or the center of their dining table.

That is the charm of the home altar or prayer table or icon corner. It's *yours*. It expresses your very own personality and aesthetic. Don't be afraid to explore what that means for you. Keeping in mind the few principles that we have tried to enunciate to help you, it will be lovely and a real expression of your family's devotion.

THE LITURGICAL YEAR

*So teach us to number our days that
we may get a heart of wisdom.*

Psalm 90:12

Have you ever thought about how we experience time? Time is something we take for granted yet is so mysterious. God's plan is revealed in time. Not only in the fullness of time, but in the gift of time itself. It is a gift, as it is a creation of God, and the dimension in which we go about receiving redemption.

What could God mean for us, to number our days?

We know someone whose sect doesn't hold with the celebration of feasts. No festivity for Christmas. None for Easter. To a Catholic who greets every saint's day as if it's the last chance to eat a celebratory bowl of ice cream, this

is unimaginable. It makes you start thinking through the different kinds of time that God gives us.

He could have given us, simply, a day, if He thought that a day is what we needed for our sanctification. But then He would have limited our perception of time to that span, wouldn't He have? In other words, we would always think about time as comprising a day. A week, a month, a season, a year—all would be unknown to us, simply because they would be superfluous to what was required for our nature.

Every day would be enough. We'd wake up every morning with a renewed spirit. We would

experience the challenges of each twenty-four-hour period without reference to any other changes. In the evening, we'd ask for forgiveness for the ways we had strayed when we were awake, and then we'd retire. We'd speak of being so many thousands of days old! If we wanted to celebrate, we'd not have much time to prepare, really.

Of course, sometimes a day is enough — is all we can apprehend. "Sufficient unto the day is the evil thereof" (Matt. 6:34, Douay-Rheims). A good part of what we know to be true is contained in those words — that there is no use worrying about tomorrow or crying over yesterday. And, of course, there will come a day when a day is all we have left.

But that can't be the whole story.

If it were, there would be no need for the week, with its seven days, the uphill climb of work, and then the mercy of rest on Sunday. A week is quite mysterious, by the way, and surely points to the truth of the unique character of Sunday, for whatever would possess all peoples to bunch their days together this way? It seems so arbitrary. Why not three days or four? Surely that is more suited to the primitive (and by extension, presumptively infantile, unsophisticated) mind, which, as the psychologist Jean Piaget has shown, doesn't count beyond that low number. Or why not count the days by ten, to match the fingers? (Perhaps the Chinese went in this direction, but not for long.) Even given the lunar calendar — which even the Babylonians found only awkwardly lined up with a division of seven, yet they persisted — other numbers seem just as workable if we're breaking things up. And yet, seven it is.

There would be no need for the four seasons of the year, with their rhythm of growth, bounty, fading glory, and cold death. Without the seasons — without at least the idea of the seasons for those who don't have four — there would be no mirror of our spiritual life in the nature we see all around us.

And then there would not be the year, with its cycle that resolves into a spiral, going ever upward toward the light of man's span on earth. Recurrence yet forward motion.

Every year brings its reminder of what happened at this time last year. The reminder gladdens our hearts or renews mourning, as the case may be. We reflect more deeply on just *what* this birth of a long-awaited child meant to us, or just *how* we were, at the time, stunned by a departure. Above all, we contemplate the events of salvation in order, with Christ in the center, yet ever renewing.

And that reflection deepens our awareness and our gratitude and our sorrow and our resolve.

But this deepening isn't meant to occur only on the personal level. We see whole nations celebrating an event—say, victory over a foe—with the healing that remembrance brings.

The Church does this for us as well in her celebrations of the hours, the week, and the liturgical year. Our little oratory can help us follow her. In our home, we will keep alive the mystery that the Church is ever presenting to us.

Here, in this chapter, we'll limit ourselves to observing the liturgical seasons at the prayer table. The possibilities would expand beyond the scope of this book if we included the many customs the family can take part in to celebrate the liturgical year in the home; not to mention those your authors aren't familiar with! After our discussion here and in the next chapter, though, we'll try to speak of the most popular devotions that could be called extra-liturgical.

But you will get the idea. The Church is our teacher—we are just giving you a basic template for your own creative response.

THE DAY WITH ITS HOURS

The book of Genesis speaks of "evening and morning, the first day," which seems to point to night, really. Think of sleep. It's a bit like not being created yet. It's also a bit like death. How you look at sleep depends, perhaps, on whether you see it as what comes before you start your day or what comes when you are finished with it.

In any case, morning comes with its promise of a new day. Every hour goes by, and it's an hour that has been lived before by all of humanity (including our Lord)—that is to say, noon happens the same way every day. Yet, it's also a new hour that has never been seen.

A day is a unit of sanctification. In the next chapter, we'll explain specifically how the Church lives these hours, called the Liturgy of the Hours—her liturgical prayer. This treasury of the Liturgy of the Hours covers all the other sorts of time as well—how to live them, how to sanctify them. We just give you an overview here, and then you can dive in.

THE WEEK — SUNDAY

In the secular world, the week is viewed as Monday, terrible, inexorable, challenging, anxiety-provoking; Wednesday, hump day; Thank God It's Friday; Saturday, the day for Taking Care of It All, although we may just sleep late due to TGIF; and Sunday, Another Day for Taking Care of It All (especially if we spent Saturday recovering).

But here is a Christian way of looking at the week. Monday through Saturday, we work with varying degrees of intensity, because God has given us the whole of creation to sanctify, giving matter its nobility. Pope John Paul II speaks of how "work is a good thing for man—a good thing for his humanity—because through work man *not only transforms nature*, adapting it to his own needs, but he also *achieves fulfillment* as a human being and indeed, in a sense, becomes 'more a human being'" (*Laborem Exercens* 9).

The Holy Father then warns about man losing his dignity if work is used against him. That can take place in two ways, it seems. One is by outside force, when man works not out of freedom but in slavery; the other comes from within, through his own inability to rest.

Sunday is the remedy for this loss of dignity. Even the poorest person can rest on Sunday and can become a philosopher—that is, one who loves the wisdom and that which is good! He rises above his day-to-day needs and simply enjoys what is given to him out of the gratuitous love of the Creator.

The source of this enjoyment and even celebration is worship. Therefore, who would not put Sunday worship, the Mass, in the very first place in his life?

If you put Sunday worship and Sunday rest first, all will be added unto you. You will finally understand life and your place in it. You will see your way clear to solutions to problems that have seemed intractable, or you will be content with the way things are, depending on what God's will for you is—which you will grasp.

When a person orients himself to Sunday and is determined to make it a different day (not another day of achieving things or getting things done), he finds that he is at peace.

As our faith grows, we see that we need more than an hour in church on Sunday. Not that we need to spend more time in the building, but that somehow the Sunday reality must permeate our daily life.

The prayer table is a way to bring the Sunday worship with its deep connection to the eternal into the home, extending it throughout the week, anchoring family life in the Eucharistic celebration. It's the physical connection between the altar in the church and the altar of the heart.

THE LITURGICAL SEASONS

Then there is the year. Every year is the same, yet every year brings us closer to our home in heaven. The Church has divided the year into liturgical seasons, each with its own flavor, so to speak. The little oratory helps us live the liturgical year with the Church.

Many parents today search for meaningful ways to convey the richness of the Faith to their children, not realizing that the celebration of the liturgical year, plain and simple, with the Church, is the best way to teach them. And it requires little more than just living along with her. Sure, there are crafts and books and various activities, but the core of liturgical living, as practiced for two millennia now, is what we ought to be after.

In this way we start thinking with the mind of the Church, because her mind is in the seasons. You will find this out as you implement this "seasonal" way of thinking — you will notice a change in the readings and the prayers at Mass, and your prayer table will often reflect that change in a natural and almost effortless way. You will become detached from the frantic way of "celebrating" that the world

pushes on us, which is focused on commerce, and attach yourself to the calm, truly joyful way of Mother Church.

Advent

The Church calendar begins with Advent, the time to prepare for the moment when heaven and earth reunite in the Incarnation. Your liturgical-year education begins here, because immediately you will notice how differently the Church enters this season from everyone else. If you can quiet your soul and turn away from the "holiday hype" of the world, you will begin to acquire the education in beauty and wonder that this season inaugurates.

The Church building is quite bare. The songs sung at Mass are full of longing; they are not the fulfilled, triumphant Christmas carols but the expectant chants of waiting. We are waiting for Christmas, that is to say, the birth of the Lord of Creation, and creation is waiting as well.

A crèche may be set up, but the Infant is not there yet. The trees may be placed before the sanctuary as the season progresses, but they are not decorated, and their plainness emphasizes the darkness. There is a penitential side to these preparations. It is the penance of expectation —the willingness to forego celebration until the moment, prepared from the beginning, arrives. One's mind turns to the poor and the help they need to stay warm and to celebrate as well. Extra good deeds are done to ready the heart to receive its Savior.

You note the Advent wreath with its four candles, lit week by week. You follow the readings as they lead from darkness into light.

At home, too, the prayer table can be made simple. Usually families put the wreath on the dining room table (or suspend it above the table from a chandelier with ribbons, as we do). Each Sunday another candle is lit, with the children taking turns. The candles can be lit every evening at dinner. A wonderful chant to sing while lighting is "O Come, O Come, Emmanuel," with its many verses. On December 17, one week before Christmas, it's traditional to sing a certain O Antiphon (verse) each day leading up to the vigil (the evening before the holy day). (See the resources for the Catholic Culture website.)

Perhaps a small nativity set can be placed on the home altar, with its Baby Jesus safely tucked away until Christmas (we put the figure in the top drawer of the dining room sideboard).

Near the nativity scene (either here or on the mantelpiece, for instance), you can place a small bowl or cup containing bits of straw. Your children can be encouraged to do little acts of service for family members and little acts of self-denial to prepare for the Lord's coming at Christmas. Explain to them that these deeds make Jesus' bed softer and that they can place a piece of straw in the manger (quietly and secretly, on their honor) for each such deed they perform. On Christmas Eve, after they have gone to bed, you can place the Infant Jesus on the bed of straws, made soft by the good deeds of your family.

Christmas

The liturgical season of Christmas begins at the Vigil Mass on Christmas Eve and continues until the feast of the Baptism of the Lord (January 9) at least, although some continue until the feast of the Presentation (February 2 — giving you more leeway on getting the tree down!). This is in stark contrast to the world, which abruptly cuts its "holiday" cacophony off on December 25, leaving folks somewhat bereft even of their ersatz celebration.

But Christians keep the feast for the octave (eight days) and beyond. At Mass, carols are sung, which is wonderful, since the repertoire is vast and certainly bears up to many days of exploration. If children are to know this treasury, it must be sung! Family visits and gatherings can continue all through the real Christmas season, with singing encouraged.

At the prayer table, the nativity has its Baby Jesus, and the Wise Men commence their journey toward the Holy Family. The Wise Men figures may be placed elsewhere in the room and, each day from Christmas to Epiphany, moved closer to the nativity scene. Children delight in moving them forward. The Holy Family icon can be brought out and a candle lit before it.

Epiphany

Epiphany, or Little Christmas, as Europeans call it, is a time of contemplating dedication to the star, which we can think of as the guide on the journey. Traditionally celebrated on January 6, this day is now moved to the second Sunday after Christmas. It can be thought of as a season that extends Christmas to feast of the Presentation. It is a time that people seem predisposed to make resolutions and recommit to their priorities.

At the prayer table, the Wise Men reach the crèche, bearing their gifts. Children can begin the challenge of thinking about vocation—the specific way they follow the call of Jesus. Gently, the prayers and readings in the Liturgy direct our minds toward the necessity of going down deep in our faith.

By February 2, the feast of the Presentation of Jesus in the Temple, the season draws to its close. Interestingly, this feast day brings many strands of contemplation together. It is also the feasts of the Purification of Mary (which makes us ponder her purity and her role as Christ-bearer) and Candlemas (which helps us consider Jesus as Light of the World). In one (of the five!) prayers from the old Latin

rite for Candlemas, we hear, "As these tapers burn with visible fire and dispel the darkness of night, so may our hearts with the help of thy grace be enlightened by the invisible fire of the splendor of the Holy Ghost, and may be free from all blindness of sin. Clarify the eyes of our minds that we may see what is pleasing to thee and conducive to our salvation. After the dark perils of this life let us be worthy to reach the eternal light."

The day resonates with the words of Simeon when Jesus was presented in the Temple by the Holy Family:

> Lord, now you let your servant
> go in peace,
> your word has been fulfilled:
>
> my own eyes have seen the salvation,
> which you have prepared in
> the sight of every people:
>
> a light to reveal you to the nations
> and the glory of your people Israel.
> (Nunc Dimittis, Luke 2:29–32)

To appreciate fully this wonder, we can even consider the way the candle is made. Dom Prosper Guéranger, O.S.B., in his *Liturgical Year*, explains:

> According to Ivo of Chartres [seventh century], the wax, which is formed from the juice of flowers by the bee, always considered as the emblem of virginity, signifies the virginal flesh of the Divine

Infant, who diminished not, either by His conception or His birth, the spotless purity of His Blessed Mother. The same holy bishop would have us see, in the flame of our Candle, a symbol of Jesus who came to enlighten our darkness. St. Anselm, Archbishop of Canterbury, speaking on the same mystery, bids us consider three things in the blessed Candle: the wax, the wick, and the flame. The wax, he says, which is the production of the virginal bee, is the Flesh of our Lord; the wick, which is within, is His Soul; the flame, which burns on top, is His divinity.

Plan ahead for your candle needs, and stock up on votive and taper candles—possibly on sale on the post-holiday clearance racks. Bring a good supply in a big basket to be blessed in church on Candlemas. If no Candlemas service is offered near you, ask the priest at a regular Mass to bless your candles. Then keep the blessed candles handy for your little oratory. If the candles are blessed, lighting one is a means of grace—prayer *of the whole Church* for the home and everyone in it.

Lent

The little oratory again reflects the plainness of the penitential season. Lent's penitence is of a different tenor from that of Advent: it's the season of real sorrow for the human condition of sin, slavery, and death, and the genuine desire for reparation that comes with the weariness of striving.

Families have different ways of living the season of Lent. The prayer table helps us decide what is most meaningful. The spiritual focus of Lent is the threefold plan of prayer, fasting, and almsgiving.

• *Prayer.* Our family has used this time to learn a new devotion (it's a good time to start saying the Rosary as a family if you don't have this habit) or to pray Vespers together. It takes a strong commitment to "begin again" if you don't have the custom of all praying together, and Lent offers a starting point.

Most parishes offer the traditional devotion of the Stations of the Cross every Friday during Lent. Sometimes with small children you won't be able to get to church for this, or perhaps you want to add the Stations on another day at home. One family we know made a "Stations log candelabra" for the prayer table, with fourteen candles, to be extinguished one by one as the Stations are prayed.

• *Fasting.* Lent begins a journey with Jesus' "Man shall not live by bread alone" (Matt. 4:4) as he wrestles with the devil in the desert. On Ash Wednesday, at the start of Lent, the Church challenges us to strengthen our will by denying ourselves. By the end of Lent, step after step, she takes us to the point where we realize that we cannot even deny ourselves without grace. After forty days of trying, more or less, we come to the Passion ready to see our unreadiness, prepared to confront our neediness.

Fasting is the main way to undertake penance. There are many ways to fast, starting with the required days of eating only one main meal on Ash Wednesday and Good Friday. In America, Catholics give up meat on Fridays during Lent, and many families add another day during the week to go without meat or eat more simply—for instance, a soup night.

We can fast from television, movies, video games, desserts and sweets, swearing, social media, and other distractions. We can fast from vices, and we can fast from good and pleasant things just to grow in the habit of doing without, of relying more on grace alone.

Lent is also a good time to grow in a habit that we'd like to acquire, such as daily Scripture reading or a certain work of mercy. Children can be encouraged to sacrifice for their siblings, offering each other coveted seats in the car or larger portions or whatever it is that they usually argue over.

Some families have a jar into which they put a bean for every act of penance they perform (and the prayer table might be a good place for this jar): a cross word not spoken, a difficult chore done without complaining, a treat passed by. On Good Friday, a dish is made with the beans!

Almsgiving. On the prayer table can also be kept a jar to put change and money saved by giving up desserts or meat on certain days in addition to Fridays. At the end of the season, the money can be donated to a worthy charity or put in the parish poor-box collection.

Holy Week

The devotions of Lent are capped by Holy Week, when preparations for Easter are mingled with an ever-deepening awareness of our spiritual journey. Palm Sunday brings its palms, which certainly can be placed on the home altar, later to be returned to the church for next year's Ash Wednesday ashes, burned at home in the fireplace, or placed in a garden bed. Holy Thursday commemorates the institution of the Eucharist and the priesthood at the Last Supper. On Good Friday we follow Jesus in His Passion. There are church services for these days, of course, but prayer time in the little oratory—even a moment resting there—helps us to internalize all these events.

Easter

Like Christmas, this feast is more than a day! The world doesn't quite know what to do with it, so to those without faith, Easter is little more than a pastel-colored blip on the calendar, half-heartedly acknowledged with an eye to selling a few cards and stuffed bunnies. But to the one following Christ's footsteps through the year, nothing compares to Easter! It takes a full fifty days (topping Lent's forty) to celebrate.

At the prayer table, the glory of the Liturgy is prolonged in the Liturgy of the Hours. Each day in the Easter Octave is the Easter Day—a Sunday—a feast, a day in the heaven of eternal joy with the resurrected Lord.

If the children decorate eggs they are especially proud of, these could be put in a glass bowl in the little oratory.

The icon corner can display an egg-shaped icon of our Lady offering us her risen Son, or another icon of the Resurrection. This event, unfortunately, is susceptible to the most terrible depictions—the failure of the artistic imagination is nowhere (except possibly in images of the Sacred Heart) so visible. For the sake of the formation of our children's conception of Christ the suffering man, a manly yet suffering God Incarnate, it's really important to avoid effeminate pictures and statues that show a resurrected Christ with no wounds (which would be unbiblical) or a Christ who is more like a dime-store angel than the Son of God. We don't want to show a Jesus whose sufferings were just a pretense, leaving no lasting impression. Icons really do help here.

Pentecost

Of course, this feast is all about the formation of the Church around the Apostles at the coming of the Holy Spirit. At the prayer table, the family can sing the Veni Creator Spiritus.

> At the Feast of Pentecost I take the sacred Book in my hands and turn eagerly to the first page of the Old Testament, and then to the first page of the New.

The first page of the Old Testament describes the creation of the world, saying that "the Spirit of God was moving on the waters." This refers to the whole universe, the seas and land masses, the animal, vegetable and mineral kingdoms: a triple realm, a manifold order; and it refers also to the governments of men, of races, peoples and tribes, inspired and moved by energies common to all mankind, and to the history of humanity slowly evolving through the centuries according to a Divine plan.

All nature, then, belongs to the temporal order, but always in the sight of God and subject to His power. (Reflection of Pope John XXIII on Pentecost)

Just as, having lived through Lent and Easter, we are utterly plunged into the life, death, and Resurrection of the Second Person of the Holy Trinity, so during Pentecost we get a living tutorial on the Third Person, the Holy Spirit. As each liturgical season arises, we experience tremendous gratitude and relief for the wisdom of this plan in time, which brings us the reminders that we need.

THE LITURGICAL SEASONS EXPAND OUR HORIZON OF FAITH

Anyone who becomes frustrated by his limitations in the face of the vastness of the truths of the Faith should remember that salvation is a true story, a narrative that unfolded in history and continues to unfold in his life. The liturgical year doesn't just enhance our participation in the big moments of that narrative — it layers all the elements in a yearlong chronicle that we can take part in as the situation allows.

Some years, for instance, when a baby is on the way, or a new job is taking up all our available energy, the big moments are all we can handle. In other years, our own personal "Ordinary Time," when, for instance, we're in the thick of trying to educate our growing children, as a family we delve into every detail of that story.

When we think of time as a gift and a way to increase devotion to God, some traditions make more sense. Suddenly they don't seem mindlessly complicated. Each of us will have a very personal list of devotions we would like to keep alive in our consciousness, but if choosing seems overwhelming, we can relax in the thought that tradition has already provided a gentle way to cycle through different aspects of religion. Time has done this for us.

Time continues to unfold in its spiral way, and we can revisit all the necessary thoughts and spiritual aids in order. If we miss something this day or week or year, we will be given an opportunity in the next. Rather than worrying that we have forgotten something, or, worse, realizing that we, in our limited nature, have simply failed to consider part of our Faith, all

the aspects are presented to us in this gift of time, which can be represented in the little oratory.

The more you find out about it, the more you appreciate how intimate and comprehensive it is!

FEAST DAYS

"Ointment and perfumes rejoice the heart: and the good counsels of a friend are sweet to the soul" (Prov. 27:9).

Just as the seasons bring us into the "year of grace," so the celebration of the saints' lives is indispensible for our humanity. We need to commemorate those who have gone before — whose virtue and strength give us the example we need. Everyone needs a friend.

Without friends, we can't live — not as real human beings in relation to each other.

The saints are our friends par excellence. They go before us and encourage us. Their friendship is marked by this quality, the very epitome of the meaning of the word *friend*: they bring us closer to Jesus Christ.

Who wouldn't celebrate the feast day of a friend? Celebrating feast days satisfies a deep need of ours — to rejoice and be glad in companionship. The Church offers feasts and memorials of the saints in her liturgical calendar. It's up to the family and the community to decide which of these to commemorate and how. We're probably all familiar with celebrations of

St. Anthony or St. Joseph in Italian sections of cities, but did you know that your family can do the same at home? Whichever saints' days and feasts appeal to you can be marked by a cake, a special supper, or a treat that you don't usually have.

At the prayer table, put an icon or prayer card of the saint for the day if you have one, perhaps with a little flower in a vase. If you are very lucky, maybe you have a relic of the saint to venerate! (Acts 19:11–12: "And God did extraordinary miracles by the hands of Paul, so that handkerchiefs or aprons were carried away from his body to the sick, and diseases left them and the evil spirits came out of them.")

This, then, is an overview of the sorts of time God has given us in His Church and in creation. Next we will look more in depth into *hours* with the marvelous prayer of the Liturgy, the Liturgy of the Hours.

On Learning to Pray
with a Breviary

Rejoice always, pray constantly, give thanks in all circumstances; for this is the will of God in Christ Jesus for you."

1 Thess. 5:16–18

Every liturgical celebration, because it is the action of Christ the priest and of his Body, which is the Church, is a sacred action surpassing all others. No other action of the Church can equal its efficacy by the same title and to the same degree.

Sacrosanctum Concilium 7

The list of the number of things Catholics are bound to do, called precepts, may astonish you by its small size. The word *precept* may not sound very approachable, but parameters are so helpful. We like to know where we stand!

Because of God's graciousness, these duties can be the seed from which the beautiful and sturdy plant of our faith flourishes. (This book is written for those who, like us, have experienced the desire to do more than this necessary minimum.) Let's list these precepts as they appear in the *Catechism of the Catholic Church*. (It goes without saying that we are all bound by the Ten Commandments.)

1. You shall attend Mass on Sundays and holy days of obligation and rest from servile labor.

2. You shall confess your sins at least once a year.

3. You shall receive the sacrament of the Eucharist at least during the Easter season.

4. You shall observe the days of fasting and abstinence established by the Church.

5. You shall help to provide for the needs of the Church, according to your ability. (CCC 2042)

The *Catechism* says, "The precepts of the Church are set in the context of a moral life bound to and nourished by liturgical life. The obligatory character of these positive laws decreed by the pastoral authorities is meant to guarantee to the faithful the very necessary minimum in the spirit of prayer and moral effort, in the growth in love of God and neighbor" (CCC 2041).

There are two more precepts (as one might expect, the number seven being a more fitting one for a list like this one than the number five) that are traditionally included in the list,

although they are treated elsewhere in the *Catechism*:

6. To obey the laws of the Church concerning Matrimony.

7. To participate in the Church's mission of evangelization of souls (in the missionary spirit of the Church).

Even these very basic requirements of being a Catholic are centered on our worship of God in the Liturgy and flow from it as a consequence.

Each of us will develop a personal plan, often called a *rule of life*, with this foundation.

Now that we've considered the beauty of the Church's liturgical year, we can see that anything we add will be helpful insofar as it keeps us in tune with her liturgical life.

Here is a good list that expands on the precepts:

• Daily Mass and the Liturgy of the Hours

• Personal prayers, including vocal prayer and silent mental prayer, and devotions ordered to the Liturgy and the seasons

• The study of Scripture

• Almsgiving

• Fasting and feasting

• Frequent Confession (the saints advise receiving the sacrament of Reconciliation once a month as a devotion to increase virtue)

GRADUALLY BEGIN A SPIRITUAL LIFE THAT INCLUDES THE LITURGY OF THE HOURS

A priest friend has commented that "the Mass is a jewel in its setting, which is the Liturgy of the Hours; all of Sacred Liturgy is a jewel in its setting, which is the cosmos."

We extend our participation in the Mass in incalculable ways. The Liturgy of the Hours is, you might say, the "setting" of the jewel of the Mass, in which God gives us union with Him in the Holy Eucharist. This union, by grace, can be carried out through the day in our personal prayer.

We can also find this union in the pattern of prayer given to us in the Liturgy of the Hours, the official corporate prayer of the Church, with deep Jewish roots in the ancient recital of the whole cycle of psalms. We need prayer in all its forms. We need to speak with God and to be silent so that He can speak to us.

In essence, the Liturgy of the Hours is the marking of certain times of day by the singing of the psalms and canticles, hymns and Scripture readings, and readings from the works of the Church Fathers. It can be thought of as an extension of the Eucharistic celebration throughout the day, and its purpose is to sanctify the whole range of human activity — and make it graceful.

We know from history and from Scripture that our Lord Himself prayed the Psalms as an observant Jew. We know from the Acts of the Apostles that His disciples continued the practice. Thus, the Divine Office has always been part of the worship of the Church in some form. It is a wonderful prayer for laypeople and for families, and we will devote a whole section of this book to its place in the Domestic Church.

In 1970 the Liturgy of the Hours was reformed, in part so that laypeople would pray it more. Pope Benedict XVI said: "I would like to renew my call to everyone to pray the psalms; to become accustomed to using the Liturgy of the Hours, Lauds, Vespers, and Compline" (Wednesday Audience, November 16, 2011).

You can find these Hours in the book of the Liturgy of the Hours, which is called the Breviary.

BEGIN WHERE YOU ARE

This chapter will take you through the idea of praying these prayers on your own and with others. We must all start from where we are, spiritually, and anything new should be introduced gradually with all our duties (including all the time and energy requirements of our station in life, such as the care of young children) in mind. So don't try to do everything! We encourage you to do what you can in a way that won't leave you feeling overwhelmed.

Consider asking the help of a trusted spiritual director—usually a priest or a religious (a monk, a friar, or a nun).

Even though one could sing all eight of the Divine Offices in a day, very few people who are not priests or religious are going to do all of that ever, and even those who do a large portion of the Office usually have started with one. Soon whatever portion you decide upon will be an ingrained habit that will seem natural. This may take months, because at first things seem awkward. And it may be years, if ever, before you expand the schedule beyond Lauds and Compline. The motivation to do more should be desire, not any sense of guilt that you *ought* to be doing more.

If it doesn't seem right after giving it a reasonable attempt, then simply stop. A good rule of thumb might be to try something new—one thing—in the spiritual realm for thirty days. This is long enough to overcome the natural inertia that resists regular practice and to discover whether the practice bears fruit. In matters involving personal preference (as opposed to precepts), it is legitimate to conclude that after allowing for normal difficulties, if something—even something undeniably good like an Office—doesn't suit you after a good trial, it's probably not right for you. It could be that doing it another way, or at another pace, or at another time of life will succeed, but for now, just don't worry and move along to something else.

WHY BOTHER WITH THE LITURGY OF THE HOURS?

The Church encourages us to pray the Liturgy of the Hours. It is the prayer prayed by Christ and the Apostles; praying it is an imitation of their example. It's a gift.

If your experience is like ours, when you start praying with your Breviary, you'll feel a change. Each day seems to get better. Things seem to go more smoothly; or if they go wrong, there's a sense of what to do about it. Even if there is something you can't change about your life, you can accept it more peacefully. If you are like us, you'll have a sense of being guided.

Among other things, the Divine Office helps release us from self-centered prayer, especially prayer during which we watch ourselves to discover any effects. Perhaps you have experienced this: the sensation of trying to gauge whether your prayer has been holy enough, eloquent enough, and so on, and whether you are right to congratulate yourself or saddened by your distraction. In the end, we feel not holy at all, and that distracted prayer has been a waste of time.

There's no need to spiral down into discouragement. Using the words of Scripture and being able to have confidence in the Church's sure hand in guidance, we can simply pray. No particular merit of ours attaches to the words—they are God's own words! No need to daydream about whether our prayer has risen above self-centeredness.

There is a way out of all this self-assessment. It is common nowadays for people to worry about having low self-esteem. According to the modern way of looking at things, we must feel good about ourselves if we are to be happy. If we have low self-esteem (which is bad, we are told), we must build ourselves up until it changes into high self-esteem (supposedly good).

Thomas Aquinas, however, thought that self-esteem was not helpful. He didn't distinguish between the high and the low; it was all bad in his eyes. The problem arises out of the very process of esteeming ourselves in the first place. Because its impulse is by its very

nature self-centered, it will inevitably lead us downward into misery. Rather than estimating our value in the eyes of God and others, we should be thinking about how we can be of service to God and to others and measuring our thoughts and actions against this standard. This idea seems to be echoed in this saying commonly attributed to St. Francis of Assisi, "It is in self-forgetfulness that we find our true selves." C. S. Lewis remarked that the humble man "will not be thinking about humility: he will not be thinking about himself at all." Praying the prayer of the universal Church helps us to cease thinking about ourselves at all.

THE STRUCTURE OF THE LITURGY OF THE HOURS AND HOW TO PRAY IT

Learning to pray the Liturgy of the Hours familiarizes us with the cycles of feasts and seasons and how to find the right prayers and readings for each one in the book. This is complicated! It's a bit like learning to drive a manual-transmission car. When you first have everything explained to you, there seem to be so many things to remember and do at once that it is almost overwhelming. However, once you become accustomed to it, driving seems so natural and straightforward that you barely need to think about it. The car almost seems to drive itself; and it's the same with the Liturgy of the Hours.

So during the learning period, don't despair. As G. K. Chesterton said, if a thing's worth doing, it's worth doing badly. We aim for perfection, but we know that in practice, the actual result is less than that! As long as we are giving it an honest attempt, we will reap the fruits.

Many variations of arrangements of the psalms have been prayed over the centuries. Different communities and times have preferences for variations that suited them while they worshipped God in a fitting way. The Rule of St. Benedict, for instance, written in the sixth century, has a weekly cycle that Benedictine monks still follow. The version that most priests pray today has a different scheme in a twenty-eight-day cycle.

There is a cyclical and mathematical pattern of beauty that can be said to govern our life on earth and to point to heaven beyond, even without our awareness of it. This pattern encompasses a sense of two-way rhythm, in which we find that everything we do enriches and is enriched by every other thing. Another pattern reflects the significance of the number seven, which relates to *covenant*, and the number eight, which relates to *perfection in Christ*.

Both of these patterns are found in the Divine Office and can help us identify a personal way of prayer that is in harmony with the divine pattern discerned in the cosmos, Tradition, and Scripture.

For more on the patterns that we find in the spiritual life, the Liturgy, and the cosmos, please see "Patterns in the Church's Liturgy" in the appendices.

FIRST, GET YOUR BREVIARY ... BUT WHICH VERSION?

To pray with the Church, use a Breviary for your region, approved by your council of bishops. Wherever you are, there will likely be a number to choose from (see the resources for recommendations). You can look at what priests and religious communities around you use; if they are in good standing with the Church and the local bishop, you can be pretty sure that laypeople can use their version legitimately too; but if you have doubts, ask at the Chancery of your diocese.

If you are praying the Office with a priest or a religious, allow him to lead the recitation or singing, and follow his choice. This is partially out of respect for the position he holds, but also because the prayer should fulfill his commitment.

LATIN OR ENGLISH?

Those who are devoted to the Extraordinary Form of the Mass might choose a Latin version approved by Pius X (just over a hundred years ago), which has 150 psalms laid out in a weekly cycle; or the older scheme set out in the Benedictine Rule, dating back to the sixth century. We should remember that to be true liturgical prayer, the translation must be approved by the bishops of the region. Many of the Latin Breviaries have a translation alongside the Latin, but if it is not approved, and we wish to be united to the Church, then we should read or sing the Latin.

We are great advocates of Latin in the Mass in the Roman Rite (which is what most Catholics belong to) whether it is the Ordinary or the Extraordinary Form. Latin ought to be the norm (as per *Sacrosanctum Concilium*, a document of Vatican II), although clearly, the vernacular is perfectly legitimate. Most of the Mass is said by the priest, which means that we can read a translation while he speaks, and much of this and the responses of the congregation are the same each week, so that the language and its meaning very quickly become familiar. If a choir or some leaders in the congregation take the responsibility for singing the responses, we can be content just to listen. Even Latin Solemn Sunday Vespers in a parish, led by the priest, with a choir singing the responses, can be highly meditative.

However, as a daily experience, with many Offices to read each day and with the text changing every time, one's Latin may not be fluent enough for it to mean very much. So, you might find it best to seek out an approved English translation for the regular daily Office..

RECOMMENDED VERSIONS IN ENGLISH

A one-volume version of the Breviary is *Shorter Christian Prayer* (Catholic Book Publishing), also known as *Christian Prayer: The Liturgy of the Hours* (Daughters of St. Paul), although the latter version is temporarily out of print.

For the complete, multivolume version, you can purchase *Liturgy of the Hours* (Catholic Book Publishing) in the United States, or *Divine Office* (Harper Collins) in the United Kingdom and the Commonwealth. These are the revised psalter of 1970 on a four-week cycle, sometimes referred to as the Paul VI psalter.

For Catholics, a very old tradition of praying the Office in English opened up with the provision for Anglicans entering the Roman Catholic Church that allows for the use of traditional Anglican texts and rites, called the Anglican Ordinariate. Because the Ordinariate has no geographic boundaries, it's an option for laypeople anywhere. The versions are the *St. Thomas More Primer* (see resources), published in the United States, and the *Customary of Our Lady of Walsingham*, published in the United Kingdom. The first is particularly useful if you want to sing. Its psalm tones and system of chant date from Catholic England; that is, before the Reformation. The adaptation is simple to use and very beautiful.

The language in these Anglican versions will appeal to some very strongly. It is redolent of the beautiful language of the King James Version of the Bible, but with modifications according to the Catholic Vulgate Bible. This is a lyrical translation, modified so that any modern reader who is not bothered by the occasional *thee* or *thou* will readily understand it. Children will benefit greatly from exposure to this beautifully reverent language.

Another possibility in English is any version of the Office produced by an Eastern Catholic church, such as the Melkite Greek Catholic Church. (Eastern Rite, as opposed to Orthodox, churches are fully in communion with Rome.)

Anglican and Eastern Breviaries tend to have fewer and longer Offices during the day but are no less liturgical for this. For Anglicans, this is a continuation of the pre-Reformation English Catholic practice of running the Offices together to allow secular priests and laypeople to sing the Office in a busy day. Choral Evensong, for example, which meant originally a song for evening (Vespers), became a combination of Vespers and Compline. If you sing these combined Offices, you can choose to mark the time for the "missing" hour with a quick prayer.

There are Internet-based versions that save the trouble of finding all the Propers for the day (those parts particular to a feast, explained later): iBreviary, DivineOffice.org, and Universalis.com are good examples.

The monthly *Magnificat* magazine is also very helpful; it's an affordable, compact, and accessible form of daily prayer (including the Mass), justly claiming that it "provides a fitting way to enter fully into the Church's liturgical rhythms and spiritual legacy."

GETTING STARTED

As an introduction to praying the Office, try starting with one or three daily offices each day —just Vespers; or Lauds, Vespers, and Compline. The single-volume Breviary or online versions will help here and allow for prayer fully united to the Church.

LAUDS, VESPERS, COMPLINE? THE NAMES AND TIMES OF EACH OFFICE

St. Benedict's Rule, which is the foundational document of monastic life in the West, lists seven Offices—or Hours—during the day and one at night: they are Lauds, Prime, Terce, Sext, None, Vespers, and Compline, with Vigils (sometimes called Matins) as the nighttime Office. Lauds is prayed at daybreak, Vespers at the beginning of the evening, and Compline at bedtime. In between Lauds and Vespers there is a series of four little offices: Prime, Terce, Sext, and None (in more recent versions, it is just the last three), which punctuate the day. Their names come from the Latin for one, three, six, and nine, indicating that they are sung at the completion of the first, third, sixth, and ninth hours of the day.

This might be a little confusing! You would think that the first hour, 1 a.m., comes in the small hours of the morning, long before Lauds. The confusion arises from the fact that time is marked differently today than it was in Benedict's day. In his time, the daylight period was divided into twelve hours, so that the beginning of the first hour was at dawn, the end of the sixth hour was at midday, and the end of the twelfth at dusk. We can immediately see a difficulty for us today. Dividing the daylight equally works somewhat in the Mediterranean region, where Benedict lived, but if we stuck to this rigidly in places further north — say, in Scotland — you would have to recalculate the hours every couple of weeks as the length of the daylight period changed.

For this and many other practical reasons, in the modern world we push daytime and nighttime together, call it all a day, and then divide it up into twenty-four equal periods, with twelve before midday and twelve afterward. A common scheme in a monastery for the Hours is Lauds around 6 a.m., Prime at 7 a.m., Terce at 9 a.m., Sext at noon, None at 3 p.m., Vespers at 6 p.m., and then Compline at 8 or 9 p.m.

There is one remaining Hour, which is for the middle of the night. Although this arises because the psalmist says we "rise at midnight" (cf. Ps. 119:62), this is not exactly what usually happens. The nighttime hour of Vigils is pushed forward so that it is done just before the "dawn" Hour, perhaps with a small break between the two.

In newer Breviaries we can see different names for the Offices. Lauds is called Morning Prayer, Vespers is called Evening Prayer, and Compline is called Night Prayer. There is a main prayer for the daytime called Prayer During the Day. Terce, Sext, and None are in an appendix at the back called Complementary Psalms. The idea is that if you say only one little Office, it can be Prayer During the Day and then, depending upon when you are able to say it, two of the Complementary Psalms, making three daytime Offices.

Vigils is now the Office of Readings. In addition to three Psalms, this Office has extended Scripture readings and a section from the writings of the Church Fathers, which is at least as long. It is a great treasure. So many of the great saints that Pope Benedict referenced in his weekly addresses during his papacy are here. We can learn from their writings, contained within the Liturgy, all about what the Liturgy is.

In the General Instruction of the Liturgy of the Hours (found at the beginning of the Breviary), we learn that the Office of Readings can be prayed at the traditional time of Vigils, before Lauds, or at any time that suits the schedule of the community or the individual. There is a Dominican community in England, for example, who say it before Prayer during the Day. It does seem beneficial to do this Office early.

INCLUDE YOUR OWN PRAYERS

The General Instruction allows for personal petitions to be added at the end of Lauds and Vespers, which is a perfect opportunity to pray for family and any communities of which we are a part. We can invoke the intercession of saints, especially those to whom we have a particular devotion.

HOW THE LITURGY OF THE HOURS REFLECTS THE CALENDAR OF SAINTS AND THE SEASONS; THE HIERARCHY OF THE DAYS

The layout of the Breviary is as follows. There is a cycle of psalms, which might be weekly or four-weekly, usually found in the middle of the book. So if you open the book at random, you might see "Sunday, Week II, Evening Prayer." This will give you the Vespers (Evening Prayer) for that day, with the psalms, canticles, hymns, and readings — perhaps referring you elsewhere in the book for those parts that are said at every

Vespers, Lauds, and Compline: the Gospel canticles (the Magnificat, the Benedictus, and the Nunc Dimittis).

This is your core Office cycle, also referred to as the Psalter. It contains the basic cycle of psalms, the foundation. However, the character of any particular day may change according to the season and the calendar of feasts. When this occurs, there are likely to be special hymns or readings or even psalms that depart from this core. So, look at the back section of the book for a calendar for the date. If there is no reference to it, it is not a feast day (a non-feast day is a ferial day). Return to the core psalter, and pray it as given. If it is a feast day, follow the additional instructions given in the calendar.

CHANGING HYMNS, PSALMS, SCRIPTURAL READINGS, AND PRAYERS

The General Instruction allows for a lot of flexibility for the choice of all texts contained within an Office. You might wonder why someone would want to change things around, but it can be helpful to have familiar texts for singing the Office. Also, you can create a bare-bones Office that can easily be photocopied to travel with.

In general, the Instruction allows for a wide interchange of psalms, provided that the character of the day and the season is maintained.

So, for example, it is permissible to exchange any psalm, hymn, or reading from one ordinary weekday Vespers for any other day's. This would allow you to create a Vespers for ordinary weekdays that was the same every day.

The Instruction stipulates that if this is done, the character of the day, relating to the feast and the season, must be preserved. Replace a Sunday Vespers hymn with another approved for Sunday Vespers. Some days, such as Easter Sunday, are so important that no substitution should be made at all.

This freedom can be helpful in the area of the hymns. There are traditional, generally four-line, hymns that were developed for the Divine Office centuries ago, sometimes called Ambrosian hymns. Chanting the Office, we find that these hymns conform to the musical unity of the Office better. The Anglicans of the nineteenth century did a lot of work to translate these hymns from the original Latin into beautiful English, retaining the original rhythmical structure. This means that we can sing these translations to the original, ancient melodies.

RIBBONS, AND THINKING OF TIME AS HAVING A *QUALITY* AS WELL AS A QUANTITY

As we consider this, it is worth remembering that a day is not just a time period. Every day has a *quality* to it, a special character that marks

it out. Although both contain twenty-four hours, a Thursday is not the same as a Friday. In the sacred cycle of time, Friday, for example, is a day when we remember Good Friday each week with self-sacrifice. (We will speak of devotions of days and months in the next chapter.)

Every day has its place in the Church's year. Is it a feast day or a fast day, and if so, why do we feast or fast on that day? The Breviary will tell us this. If there is a feast, it will tell us what we are celebrating — say, Our Lady of Sorrows — and give a little background information; and then it will tell the grade of the feast — for example, a memorial. (There are various degrees of commemoration, with lesser and higher feast days called, depending on the Breviary, *optional memorials*, *memorials*, *feasts*, and the highest, *solemnities*, which are like Sundays during the week.) Then there are days of penance, marked by self-sacrifice. These days have been assigned their particular character to commemorate significant events in the life of Christ or the anticipation of the world to come.

For each of these sorts of day, you will see instructions on psalms, readings, hymns, and so on that are appropriate to it. This might send you to three or four parts of the book, to which you must refer at the appropriate juncture within each Office. This is where all those colored ribbons dangling from the binding come in — you use them to mark those places so you know where to go at the right time (although sometimes it seems that there aren't enough ribbons!).

As well as thinking about the date, we have to think about the season. Are we in Lent, Advent, Easter, or Ordinary Time? Typically the parts for the season are in the front section, before the psalter.

Sometimes there are parts of the Office from both sections. Then we have to know which substitution has priority over the other. This depends on the season, the time within the season, and the nature of the feast; and the General Instruction tells us this.

If you are anything like us, it will take a long time and careful reading to be able to get all of this right without help from someone else. It does seem that the very process of working all of this out before you can even start is a form of meditation in itself! Do the best you can ... but do try.

As a fallback, you can always go online and see what Universalis.com has for the day (and we regularly do this). These websites take the work out for you, but it is worth at some point trying to understand how the Breviary functions. In the process of learning, you become much more aware of the different qualities of the seasons and the year. Your experience will be the richer for it.

Of course, we get a sense of our passage through sacred time by attending Mass too, for each Mass reflects the season and the day. Praying the Liturgy of the Hours amplifies this awareness. Furthermore, what the Liturgy has to teach us each day is powerfully articulated across the hours of the day.

TIME FLEXIBILITY

There is a lot of flexibility in choosing times to pray, and like so many things in the Church, principles take into account personal or group situations. So, for example, you could pray Vigils and Lauds (Office of Readings and Morning Prayer) first thing in the morning; one daytime Office mid-morning; one around noon; and one mid-afternoon. Pray Vespers sometime in the late afternoon or the early evening and then Compline toward bedtime.

Even if we have a routine in which we attempt to follow set times, we should not worry if we miss one occasionally, get to it late, or sometimes run a couple together rather than doing them separately. As laypeople, we do not take vows of obedience to a rule or a superior, so in this respect we can devise our own rule. As with most aspects of the spiritual life, guidance from a good spiritual director is helpful.

POSTURE

Man's nature consists of a profound unity of body and soul. Just as thoughts can direct the body, so the bodily attitude can affect our thoughts and feelings. Our thoughts and motives are likely to be mixed, and paying attention to what our body is doing can be helpful. On those occasions when the *feeling* of prayerfulness or peacefulness is missing, adopting a reverential posture tends to lead the heart in the right direction. Sometimes the right thoughts and feelings follow right actions.

If you visit a monastery, you will find that certain postures are adopted at certain times during the prayer. You might like to know what these are. Traditionally, we stand through the introit and hymn through the recitation of the psalms, then sit. Stand for the Gospel canticle until the close, or if there is no Gospel canticle, stand for the closing prayer. Bow in honor of the Trinity at its invocation in the last verse of each hymn and at the end of every psalm: (bow) *Glory be to the Father and to the Son and to the Holy Spirit;* (stand erect) *as it was in the beginning, is now and ever shall be, world without end. Amen.* Incline the head forward in a *slight* bow at the mention of the name Jesus.

CHANT

When we sing our prayers, we engage voice and hearing. St. Augustine famously remarked that when we sing our prayers, we pray twice: when the music is appropriate to the text, its beauty adds a dimension that words cannot. The ideal would be for us to sing the whole Liturgy. Those who are musical can go straight to the Anglican Ordinariate Breviary, which has a noble but simple form of chant that's quickly assimilated. Even if you do not use this particular Breviary, its form of chant can easily be applied to any other one.

If the very mention of singing out loud causes you anxiety, before you give up, at least read the appendix "Even You Can Sing!"

PRAY ALWAYS

The General Instruction of the Liturgy of the Hours tells us, "The purpose of the liturgy of the hours is to sanctify the day and all human activity." Every minute of the day can benefit from it. The *Catechism* tells us that "this celebration, faithful to the apostolic exhortations to 'pray constantly,' is so devised that the whole course of the day and night is made holy by the praise of God" (CCC 1174). As the world turns, someone, somewhere, is praying the Church's prayer, begging God's grace on

Ant.
vi F
R Egá-li * ex progé-ni-e Ma-ri-a ex-ór-ta re-

fulget: cu-jus pré-ci-bus nos adju-vá-ri, men-te et spi-

behalf of the whole world. We ourselves can participate!

Leaning on this prayer of the whole church, tended to by our brothers and sisters in Christ, we can profit from the words of St. Basil the Great:

> We should not express our prayer merely in syllables, but the power of prayer should be expressed in the moral attitude of our soul and in the virtuous actions that extend throughout our life … This is how you pray continually — not by offering prayer in words, but by joining yourself to God through your whole way of life, so that your life becomes one continuous and uninterrupted prayer. (homily on the martyr Julitta)

In following the pattern of the worship of the Church, we align ourselves to the liturgy in heaven and to the source of grace, God. We imbue our lives with an ordering principle that harmonizes us not only with the angels in heaven, but also with the whole of creation. There is a divine orientation that stays with us after our syllables of prayer are over. This is how the Liturgy, the sacraments, and our lives outside the church building are integrated. It is grace that makes our life one unceasing prayer.

PRAYER OF THE HEART

Let us pray with freedom, as children of God. All of these directions come together, to the degree that we engage our whole person in prayer, in praying with our heart. The heart is that place at our core, where all actions, thoughts, and feelings are taken into account, that place that represents our human center of gravity. It is where we really are. The heart is the symbol of love because love of God and man is what each person is made for — it symbolizes the ideal for man. Thus, if someone is totally committed to something, we say, "His heart is in it."

By striving for this ideal of praying with our whole person, continuously, and uniting this prayer to our whole way of life, we can perhaps begin to say that our heart is in it for God!

GETTING CLOSER TO GOD'S WORD

Thy word is a lamp to my feet and a light to my path.

Psalm 119:105

If we are to follow the direct path of Scripture and come straight to the final destination, then right from the beginning — when simple faith starts to draw us towards the light of the Father — our hearts should kneel down and ask the Father to give us, through his Son and the Holy Spirit, true knowledge of Jesus and of his love.

St. Bonaventure (Office of Readings)

Many of us Christians have good intentions to begin a study of Scripture and yet never do. In many ways the project seems overwhelming. Thus, it will come as a relief to know that the Church, like a good mother, has made it possible for us to know a lot of Scripture — in fact, to go through most of the Bible in much of a year (and more of it every three years) — just by following the Liturgy as a whole — the Mass (including daily Mass) and the Divine Office (which we will discuss in the next chapter) taken together.

Even those who don't pray the Liturgy of the Hours in full will find a good portion of Scripture by praying only the Office of Readings. Of course, the Mass itself is Scripture from beginning to end, so a good bit of it sinks in, regardless of how much we consciously set out to read or study on our own. The *Catechism* tells us that "the reading of the Word of God at each Hour ... and readings from the Fathers and spiritual masters at certain Hours, reveal more deeply the meaning of the mystery being celebrated, assist in understanding the psalms, and prepare for silent prayer" (CCC 1177).

It's clear that to love God, we must know Him, and to know Him, we would naturally want to draw closer to Him in His Word.

The document from Vatican II on the Scriptures (*Dei Verbum*) begins with the affirmation that Jesus is God's Word — the person of Jesus *is* His revelation. The Word is

everything the Church offers us: Scripture, the Church (the Body of Christ), and above all, Jesus in the Eucharist, the Word made flesh.

Knowing Jesus in His Word leads us to the full knowledge and overwhelming love of the most holy Trinity. The desires of the saints draw them toward the Trinity, in which all that is good and true is and finds its completion, as St. Bonaventure reminds us. When we know God's Word well, we find that our participation in the Liturgy — the life the Trinity shares with us — deepens as well.

So above and beyond what we find in the Liturgy, we might try to introduce the regular reading of Scripture into our prayer lives without causing too much stress. Even arriving at Mass a few minutes early, or opening the Bible on the prayer table at home, and spending a few minutes reading and meditating on Scripture can yield great results in our spiritual life.

Perhaps the ancient method of Scripture study, called in Latin the *lectio divina* ("holy reading"), might be fruitful. The *Catechism* teaches that "the *lectio divina*, where the Word of God is so read and meditated that it becomes prayer, is thus rooted in the liturgical celebration" (CCC 1177). After all, reading God's Word is different from reading other texts. It isn't just an intellectual exercise, although it will certainly be stimulating, and it isn't just a way to apprehend the beauty of truth, although we will do that as well. Reading God's Word is a way to pray, to speak to God and hear what He has to say to us. Reading Scripture is an encounter with God.

A WAY OF READING SCRIPTURE

We offer a little outline of this method here for beginners who wish to come closer to God's Word in Scripture. (Get a Bible in a beautiful and approved translation. Check the resources for recommendations.) There are four parts to the method, each of which probably takes longer to explain than to do!

- *Lectio.* The first part is the reading of the text. Select a passage to read. It does not have to be long at all. Now, very few people succeed when they start with Genesis and go right through, for the very good reason that the Bible is not one book, but rather a shelf of books. Thus, Leviticus, for instance (where many get bogged down), is a book on the shelf that contains mainly instructions for the ancient Jewish tribe of priests, the Levites. It's more than permissible—it's advisable—to skip around the books of the Bible!

Clearly, one needs a system. One system is to start with the Gospels, reading through them (including the Acts, which is often called the Gospel of the Holy Spirit), and then beginning again. Another is to read the fourteen narrative books of salvation history, which start with Genesis and end with Acts (for one such study, see the *Great Adventure* Series in the resources). Another is to pick the readings for Mass that day, consulting your missal or a website that offers that information. A perfectly acceptable system is to go directly to a bit that you already know well—say, a parable such as that of the prodigal son—and read the parts leading up to it and coming after it. You can always start at the beginning of the Gospel of Matthew and read straight through later on.

Whichever system you use, having selected the passage, say a short prayer for receptivity to God's Word. A simple "Come, Holy Spirit" will do—not necessarily the whole prayer (which you will find at the beginning of a study Bible, among other places), just that one phrase! And then read away. As phrases catch your attention, reread them. If nothing in particular jumps out, you may reread the whole allotted passage a number of times, or simply let it sink in, depending on its length. God will speak to you. Little by little, you will become aware of a whisper or an inner certainty. It may not be at the very time you are reading, but it will come. Don't worry about any lack of knowledge you may sense—God meets you where you are.

To increase your understanding, supplement your Scripture reading with commentaries (found right along with the text in study Bibles—see the resources). (Avoid any commentaries that aren't rooted in faith and loyalty to the Magisterium of the Church—her teaching authority —and to the truth that Scripture is the inspired Word of God.) The Office of Readings often supplies the breathtakingly deep commentary of the Church Fathers on a particular reading.

• *Meditatio*. The second part is thinking. Don't be confused by the word *meditation*. Today, meditating on a phrase might suggest repeating it like a mantra in an Eastern religion. In that sense, the goal is the *elimination* of thought; or at the very least, a passive process of just letting the mind drift in the ethereal breeze. This image makes it hard for some people to

know what they are supposed to be doing with Scripture—all that seems contradictory to trying to *understand* the passage, which involves bringing our reason to the text. Books you might have encountered about *lectio divina*, authored by stream-of-consciousness aficionados, might not clear up the predicament.

There is a difference in meaning between Christian and non-Christian ideas of meditation. In the Christian tradition, *meditate* means "meditate upon," which is the same as "think about." So in meditation, you do pause and allow for the prompting of the Spirit in the form of thoughts and ideas; when these occur, you ponder over them, perhaps asking: *What does this mean? Is there something that applies to me directly? How can I act on this during the rest of the day?* And so on. You can even simply ask, "Speak, Lord, for thy servant hears" (1 Sam. 3:9, NRSV). This is in contrast with the form of meditation that consists of trying to eliminate thought, which is the opposite of what we are talking of here.

• *Oratio*. This leads to the third stage, prayer. Prayer is simply conversation with God. We can ask God to show us how to act on something or for help in those areas that the meditation focused on (for instance, anger or envy). The worry might be that sometimes we don't seem to have drawn any profound lessons or thoughts to react to. A wise monk of our acquaintance offers the salutary advice that quite often this happens to him; he doesn't think it is anything to worry about. He simply praises God for this chance to hear His Word.

• *Contemplatio.* The fourth part is contemplative prayer. One might think that *contemplation* and *meditation* are two words for the same thing, but there is a difference.

In contrast to *meditatio*, this part is more receptive. It is passive only in the sense that it is a state of mind that is given to us as a gift from God. Therefore actively pursuing it cannot guarantee its occurrence. It is a state of stillness of mind, of just being with God. As a gift from God, it is given to whomsoever He pleases and for reasons beyond our understanding. Thus, we mustn't try to interpret what happens at this stage, when we've been sitting quietly, reading, perhaps studying, thinking over the text, allowing it to sink in, speaking to God (deep within ourselves) about what we've read. We cannot draw conclusions about how well we've prayed or our level of spiritual development. God either gives or He doesn't. Contemplation is not a reward automatically arising from doing the first three stages well; it is something that simply either happens or not, and over which we have no control.

You may not notice any dramatic indications of God's presence, as some holy people report. However, you can be sure that God forms the person of goodwill during this time of receptivity. Good things may be happening without our awareness, just as we see that children's bodies grow without their knowledge of the process.

You may experience moments of understanding and insight in regard to Scripture or even other areas of life; these thoughts can arise during this silent moment—or even at another time. The thought that we haven't done more than take a sip is a good one.

We leave you with some more words of encouragement:

Lord, who can comprehend even one of your words? We lose more of it than we grasp, like those who drink from a living spring. For God's word offers different facets according to the capacity of the listener, and the Lord has portrayed his message in many colors, so that whoever gazes upon it can see in it what suits him. Within it he has buried manifold treasures, so that each of us might grow rich in seeking them out. The word of God is a tree of life that offers us blessed fruit from each of its branches. It is like that rock which was struck open in the wilderness, from which all were offered spiritual drink. As the Apostle says:

They ate spiritual food and they drank spiritual drink …

Be thankful then for what you have received, and do not be saddened at all that such an abundance still remains. What you have received and attained is your present share, while what is left will be your heritage. For what you could not take at one time because of your weakness, you will be able to grasp at another if you only persevere. So do not foolishly try to drain in one draught what cannot be consumed all at once, and do not cease out of faintheartedness from what you will be able to absorb as time goes on. (St. Ephrem the Syrian, Office of Readings, Sunday, Week 6 of Ordinary Time)

DEVOTION

For the people this wisdom [of piety] is also a principle of discernment and an evangelical instinct through which they spontaneously sense when the Gospel is served in the Church and when it is emptied of its content and stifled by other interests.

Sacrosanctum Concilium 13

In chapter 5, we really delved into the Liturgy of the Hours. In this chapter, we will discuss devotion in general, just because some devotions are traditional to family life; and some are so very near and dear to the hearts of the faithful, springing as they do from their piety, and thus have a place in the little oratory. (In the next chapter we will speak more of the most beloved of these: the Rosary.)

For laypeople (that is to say, those of us with the vocation to live in the world, transforming it with love, primarily through the gift of the family according to God's plan in marriage), to pray the Liturgy of the Hours is a matter of complete freedom. We've tried to outline ways to incorporate the richness of the Liturgy into daily life. The little oratory seems to help with this.

Lived in its simplest way, the little oratory provides a place to say morning and night prayers, framing the day, and to live the seasons in ways that are traditional and worth knowing about. Keep in mind the discussion of the liturgical year in chapter 4. It's by our participation in the Liturgy—which has at its center the Eucharist, Jesus Himself—that we find our efforts sanctified. Ultimately, our aim is to offer our devotion (in church and out) to the Blessed Trinity.

MORNING AND NIGHT

The Morning Offering

This prayer, which we can teach in a simple form to our children, enables us to offer the whole day to God. I'm sure we've all experienced the dismay of realizing that whole chunks of time have gone by without our realizing it or without our having lifted our hearts to God at all. Or something intense happens—an accident or a sudden blow—and later we notice that our reaction was quite completely, shall we say, secular in nature, or maybe even profane.

The Morning Offering consoles us, because at the beginning of the day we offered the whole thing, with all its works, sufferings, prayers, and joys, to God. It's an efficacious consecration! Regardless of whatever failings we stumble into later, it's a done deed.

Here is a form that children can memorize easily:

O Jesus, through the Immaculate Heart of Mary, I offer You my prayers, works, joys, and sufferings of this day, for all the intentions of Your

Sacred Heart, in union with the Holy Sacrifice of the Mass throughout the world, in reparation for my sins, for the intentions of all my relatives and friends, and in particular for the intentions of the Holy Father. Amen.

If we say the Morning Prayer of the Liturgy of the Hours, we are making our Morning Offering and don't need to repeat this formula.

Nightly examination of conscience

Some families stand at the prayer table and say night prayers together. Probably many more kneel at the foot of a child's bed to do this. You can see that it might be lovely to have a small icon corner or some sort of shelf with images to make a little prayer corner for your children's room.

In any case, even if there is just a crucifix above the bed, the attention of the children is drawn to it. When they are very little, they will simply recite some prayers of thanksgiving and protection during sleep. Each child may ask God to bless those he loves. Since the prayers of children are highly pleasing to God (Matt. 18:10; 19:14), it's a good idea to have them pray for the needs of others.

As they get older and become aware of their own shortcomings, they experience real contrition and shame. Parents have the delicate undertaking of helping their children enter into the "interior castle," as St. Teresa calls it, of their own inner life with God. They also start to have a sense of the day as a unit of grace, each day bringing its sorrows and joys.

This is a step-by-step process that the adults are always learning as well, so it's good to go over it and think of each aspect, gently helping the children to understand each one. This understanding unfolds over a long period, so take it as slowly as you see it being absorbed — no faster!

As a parent, you will notice your child showing gratitude spontaneously for "a good day." St. Ignatius taught us that a good examination of conscience starts with just this — deep thanksgiving, not only for any wonderful things that occurred, but also for the gift of life itself.

Then we are to see ourselves as God sees us. On this day, was He pleased with us, with what we did and failed to do? Said? Thought? It takes just a quick glance over each part of the day and isn't meant to be an exhaustive, tedious search. Quietly, in our own heart, God will whisper what wasn't good and what needs to be worked on.

The *examen*, as this particular look into things is called, will then naturally include sorrow and a plea for forgiveness and mercy. Of course, we all know that it's futile to be sorry for something without the intention of changing the habit of doing it. A firm purpose of amendment makes an amazing difference. Even where the habit recurs, it's the willingness to try again to do better that pleases God.

Whereas, if we content ourselves with a hopeless admission of guilt, how can He help us? Thus, the good parent guides the child to choose something specific to work on. Not "I will be better tomorrow," but "I will, with Your help, try to be generous with my toys."

Great conversations arise when we lead a child in this matter of examining his conscience. You will see that as he approaches the time for his first Holy Communion, preparing this way in family prayer, with loving guidance from Mother and Father, he will be ready for his first Confession. Without too much technical catechesis, he learns the difference between venial sins (those that arise from human weakness and make us less loving) and mortal sins (those that, because they involve the consent and knowledge of the person doing them and are serious in nature, deal the soul a killing blow — see 1 John 5:16–17). Even a child begins to see the need to kneel before the man consecrated by God to forgive sins in His name (because, although only God can forgive sins, He has bestowed this power on His priests — see John 20:21–23).

And it's interesting how all this, simply explained to a child, sheds light on our own interior struggle.

At some point, the night prayer should include an Our Father, the prayer Jesus Himself taught us. All this, taking so long to write out and explain, even in outline form, is the work of a few minutes every night.

So the Morning Offering and the night prayers are a perfect place to start a prayer life with children in the little oratory.

TIME CAN INCREASE DEVOTION

Here are some traditional devotions attached to particular days of the week and to individual months.

Days of the week
You probably already know that the different Mysteries of the Rosary are said on different days (the Joyful Mysteries on Mondays and Saturdays; the Sorrowful Mysteries on Tuesdays and Fridays; the Luminous Mysteries on Thursdays; and the Glorious Mysteries on Sundays and Wednesdays). We will go into more depth about the Rosary in the next chapter, but for now, you might not know that the days also have their special emphasis, in tradition, on various truths of the Faith. This can be very helpful if we are feeling spiritually dry on a particular day.

Sunday—the Resurrection, the Trinity. Sunday is a day of rest and a "little Easter"—a celebration of the Resurrection and Redemption.

Monday—the Holy Spirit; the souls in Purgatory. We should pray for our beloved dead and the dead who have no one to pray for them (2 Macc. 12:46).

Tuesday—the angels. Remember that we each have a guardian angel. Thank your angel for his protection! To know more about what the Church teaches about angels, consult the *Catechism of the Catholic Church*, 325–354.

Wednesday—St. Joseph. This is the day the week turns on. It's no wonder that the wisdom of popular piety put St. Joseph here, in the center of daily life. St. Joseph represents fatherhood, care, protection, a happy death, and sanctified work. He has been called the Shadow of the Father.

Thursday—the Blessed Sacrament. Our Lord instituted the Eucharist and the priesthood at the Last Supper.

Friday—Christ's Passion and the Sacred Heart. Our Lord suffered and died for us, which is why Catholics abstain from meat on this day and perhaps in general view it in a penitential light.

Saturday—the Blessed Virgin. An ancient devotion rooted in the Liturgy. From our perspective in a discussion of the Liturgy of the Hours, and thinking of the days of creation, it's interesting to note that by the fifteenth century, the Dominicans were speaking (and chanting) of our Lady as the one through whom salvation was accomplished — thus, the last day of creation, being fulfilled in the salvation offered by her Son, is seen as a fitting day to honor her.

Mothers especially will see how it may come about naturally, when teaching their children about the days of the week, that they raise their eyes to these supernatural thoughts on each of the days. Children love to embellish. Thinking of each day with its special character will draw them into a lively faith.

Months

The months, too, each have a character given to them by tradition, usually because of a feast day that occurs in that month. Parents can look ahead and emphasize the feast and the virtue that can be developed during that month. Spreading the devotions out this way can give us a little peace when it comes to the sheer number of devotions in the Catholic Church! Using time, we can know that we're on track and not missing anything important.

At the same time, we can be fine with letting some things go, confident that they will turn up again. This is a far better strategy than randomly trying to get all the devotions in, which would be impossible!

Do we need to do all of these? Make a point of changing themes every month? Without a doubt, no. If something strikes you, go with it. If it seems too much, don't worry. This is all offered in the spirit of "in case you are interested and the Holy Spirit is whispering to you."

January — the Holy Name of Jesus. John Paul II restored the feast of the Holy Name to January 3. It's worth looking up the origin of this feast, and contemplating the power of the Lord's Holy Name and the respect due to it. Many people try to develop the habit of bowing their head slightly whenever the name of Jesus is mentioned. If you live or work with people who tend to take the Lord's name in vain, you can respond by saying, "Bless the name of Jesus!" Even saying it internally is an act of reparation.

Or, you can do as a friend did when a fellow swore using Jesus' name. "Jack, I didn't know you were so religious!" That put a stop to it.

At the prayer table: During prayer, teach your children to bow their heads slightly when the name of Jesus is mentioned. Little by little, this practice will become second nature to them and will be a powerful witness to others.

February — the Holy Family. This devotion came about in the seventeenth century. In the words of Pope Leo XIII, "Nothing truly can be more salutary or efficacious for Christian families to meditate upon than the example of this Holy Family, which embraces the perfection and completeness of all domestic virtues."

At the prayer table: Display on your stand an icon, a statue, or a prayer card of the Holy Family.

March—St. Joseph, whose feast day is March 19. St. Joseph is the patron of the home. The more you learn about him, the deeper will your faith in God's providence go.

A beautiful devotion is to pray the Litany of St. Joseph on the seven Sundays preceding his feast day. To determine when to begin this devotion, get out your calendar, begin at March 19, and count back seven Sundays.

At the prayer table: A statue or icon of St. Joseph may be moved into prominence, and your family can pray the litany, dwelling on Joseph's titles, which are very instructive and enriching. On his feast day, much rejoicing occurs, not least because this solemnity provides a welcome relief from the fasting of Lent!

April—the Blessed Sacrament. This devotion grew in the sixteenth century. If you are trying to include visits to the Blessed Sacrament in your family life, this might be a good time to start (and you can make a special effort on Thursdays, the day devoted to the Blessed Sacrament).

Making a visit is very simple. Find a church with open doors. Go in and visit our Lord, waiting there in the tabernacle! You can do as little as just sit there with Him, keeping Him company. Some people like to say an Our Father, a Hail Mary, and a Glory Be three times, and then make a spiritual Communion: that is, to express the desire to receive Jesus in Communion at that moment and even to imagine doing so. You might pray, "Come, Lord Jesus!" or the ancient prayer: "I wish, Lord, to receive You with the purity, humility, and devotion with which your most holy Mother received You, with the spirit and fervor of the saints."

Children can be encouraged to tell Jesus quietly, interiorly, what is on their minds (although don't be surprised—be proud—if they take to showing Him a new doll or toy). And you can do the same. As Easter usually falls in April, it's the perfect time, with hardly any thought required, to contemplate the institution of the Eucharist and the devotion we should all have to it.

At the prayer table: Chant the Pange Lingua together as a family. It's nice to know by heart for the times you attend Benediction.

May—our Lady. The Easter season almost always extends into May. The primary emphasis must be on Easter, the Ascension, and Pentecost, of course, as the liturgical takes precedence over the devotional. But they are not in conflict.

As we are bringing flowers to put in vases on the prayer table, we can be speaking of the role of Mary in this season. Scripture gives us ample food for thought. Mary represents the Church, which is founded in these events. She is the Queen of the Apostles, without, as Hans Urs von Balthasar points out, herself being an apostle. Von Balthasar suggests that Mary has other, greater powers, a wonderful thought to contemplate. When we think of the Church, there are two models we can refer to—the hierarchical one (apostolic and male) and the maternal one (Marian and female).

As soon as you express it this way, it becomes clear that these models must complement and refer to each other without detriment. In fact, each model supports and enhances the other. As we contemplate Mary and her role in salvation, we begin to see, if it has been troublesome to us, what women would lose if they posited the hierarchical model as the only one worth emulating.

At the prayer table: Take all the offerings your children bring in from the garden, and put them before the icon or statue of our Lady.

Now is a good time to start the habit of praying the Rosary.

June—the Sacred Heart. The heart symbolizes love and the whole person. Jesus appeared to St. Margaret Mary Alacoque to remedy a hard, rigid practice of religion that had cooled men's sense of being created as a human person to love. When we contemplate Jesus' Sacred Heart, we are contemplating His humanity—the fact that He is God and man and has, along with His divine nature, a human nature that loved in a human way. The family especially is a manifestation of what human love can be, so this month is a gift for understanding how God wants His love to be expressed.

At the prayer table: Display an image of the Sacred Heart.

July—the Precious Blood of Jesus. St. John Chrysostom said:

> This Blood, poured out in abundance, has washed the whole world clean … This is the price of the world; by it Christ purchased the Church … This thought will check in us unruly passions. How long, in truth, shall we be attached to present things? How long shall we

remain asleep? How long shall we not take thought for our own salvation? Let us remember what privileges God has bestowed on us, let us give thanks, let us glorify him, not only by faith, but also by our very works. (Homily 46)

The whole month of July can be devoted to this Blood that saves.

At the prayer table: Pray the antiphon from the prayers for the day of the feast of the Precious Blood, maybe on all the Sundays of July.

August — the Immaculate Heart of Mary. "Mary kept all these things, pondering them in her heart." (Luke 2:19). "His mother kept all these things in her heart" (Luke 2:51). Scripture reveals Mary's heart — its purity especially (and "pure" is what the word *immaculate* means). This month we contemplate her goodness in receiving the Word, having faith, and loving God and the world enough to declare her *fiat* — her "I will do it." The big feast this month is of her Assumption into Heaven, which points to the resurrection of the body in the world to come.

At the prayer table: Display an image of our Lady's Immaculate Heart.

September — the Seven Sorrows of Mary. Contemplating Mary's Seven Sorrows that are told in Scripture — the prophecy of Simeon; the flight of the Holy Family into Egypt; the loss of the Child Jesus in Jerusalem; the meeting with Christ on the road to Calvary; the Crucifixion of Jesus; the taking down of Jesus' body from the Cross; and the burial of Jesus — leads us immediately to the sufferings of Christ. Seeing them from Mary's point of view reveals to us the depths of human sorrow. His sorrows are hers and, thus, ours.

At the prayer table: Pray the prayers of the Seven Sorrows of Mary, which you can find online.

October — the Holy Rosary, the holy angels. We knew a priest who often commented on how intimately the angels are entwined in the story of the birth of Jesus. Read the Gospels with this in mind to see what he means. We contemplate the events of Christ's conception and birth in the Joyful Mysteries of the Rosary. The whole of the Rosary is a contemplation of all the events of Christ's life and death and beyond. The feasts of the angels and of the Rosary in October make this their month.

At the prayer table: Make it a priority to pray the family Rosary this month.

November — all saints and all souls. This month we particularly remember those saints who are not necessarily mentioned by name in the roll call of the Church (the canon), but who undoubtedly exist and are close to us. They are the holy men and women whose stories may be known to only a few, or possibly to no one, but to whose faithfulness we may owe our own journey. Who knows what devoted soul prayed for you and me to love God? That person is worthy of honor. Thus, the feast of All Saints.

And then there are the beloved dead who may stand in need of our prayers. Our Lord cautioned us to judge no one's soul. Often we (correctly) interpret that to mean "judge not that a person is condemned." But the injunction also means that we ought to refrain from judging that a person is undoubtedly sanctified. It might be helpful to think of it this way: When I die, I will be painfully aware of my own shortcomings. I will desperately hope that those who care for me (and my eternal soul) will pray for me in the process of purification.

In addition to the hidden saints, there are the poor souls in Purgatory, who are the main focus and especially cared for in November. From the earliest days of Christianity, Liturgies were offered for the dead and people left prayers for the dead on monuments in the catacombs. Scripture also supports the practice of praying for the souls of the dead (2 Macc. 12:46).

We can be sure, then, that what seems to come naturally to our families—that we remember and pray for our dead—is approved by the Church. It's a good thing to have our own commemoration of relatives and friends who have passed, remembering them in our little oratory and at certain times, such as the anniversary of their death or in November.

At the prayer table: The prayer cards offered at funerals of friends and loved ones can be placed there for the month, and we can

remember to offer special prayers on behalf of those dearly departed.

December—the Immaculate Conception. Of course, December is the month of the Nativity of Our Lord. In some ways, we're so familiar with the devotion to the Nativity that we almost forget to consider what God-made-man really means for us. It's about the sanctification of creation, not only our own personal redemption. Taking on flesh—really and truly becoming a human being—means elevating to a new status the "It is good" that God proclaimed at the creation.

Our Lady is the exemplar of what this all means for us as God's creatures. The feast of her Immaculate Conception—her preservation from the condition of Original Sin—occurs in this month. It's a good time to think about how Jesus' human nature came from her—the way he looked, the way he felt. His human heart comes from Mary.

At the prayer table: At the start of Advent, a small crèche with the infant Jesus not yet placed in the manger is an object of wonder when displayed in a special place like the prayer table or the mantelpiece. Just looking at Mary and Joseph there in prayer, waiting for the Savior Child, is very moving to the whole family.

FAMILY FEAST DAYS

God's plan for us is family life—the life of His own family, Father, Son, and Holy Spirit. We are to be His adopted sons and daughters—to have a relationship with Him that is as strong as a blood relationship, with the blood being the Blood of the Lamb.

The first covenant that God made with man was to establish the family in the order of days. A man cleaves to a woman to make her his wife, so that they might have children and bring all of creation into the order of sanctification.

Thus, our daily family life is meant to be the normal way that children grow into this relationship with God. We learn to love by being loved by a mother and a father. We learn to pray with our parents. Conversation in the family builds this relationship of love, as do all the activities that we enjoy together (and even the tough bits, such as disciplining and difficulties, reveal the fidelity of God when we don't let them discourage us).

It follows that all the important dates in a family's life are feasts—as important to that particular family as any on the calendar.

Do not hesitate to celebrate them all: wedding anniversary, birthdays, baptism days, patron saints' feast days, memorials of the dates of loved ones' passing. A lovely custom is to place pictures appropriate to the day—a wedding photo or a baby picture or another family photo—on the prayer table to give honor to the person whose day it is.

Praying the Rosary

*To pray the Rosary is to hand over our burdens
to the merciful hearts of Christ and his Mother.
The Rosary does indeed "mark the rhythm of
human life," bringing it into harmony with the
"rhythm" of God's own life, in the joyful communion of the Holy Trinity, our life's destiny
and deepest longing. Through the Rosary the
faithful receive abundant grace, as though from
the very hands of the Mother of the Redeemer.*

Pope John Paul II

You might be accustomed to praying the Rosary—it's a lifelong habit, you're completely familiar with all its details, and you know how to say it in a group, particularly in a family. Perhaps you can't imagine any other communal prayer outside of the Mass that could be more fulfilling, and the Liturgy of the Hours sounds a bit suspect, like an attempt to rob the Blessed Mother of the great love she inspires.

Perhaps you have recently learned of the Rosary and would like to pray it with your family, but the obstacles are many. It seems unattainable to pray it aloud without awkwardness, and the thought of somehow getting your kids used to it couldn't be more daunting!

This chapter offers some practical ideas on how to proceed. Perhaps we can even help the lifelong Rosary pray-ers to raise things a notch.

See "Devotion to Mary (and the Saints)" in the appendices for an explanation of how the Rosary fits into the life of the Church as a devotion, whether it's absolutely required, and some quotations from documents as to its fittingness.

Popes and saints have recommended and urged the faithful, especially families, to pray the Rosary. Whole movements have been founded on it, wars won with it, and books and encyclicals written about it. We will confine ourselves to point out that the Rosary has the virtue of compressing important points of the Faith and the history of salvation into one easily memorized devotion. This makes it ideal for those on the road, those who can't access their Breviaries, those who are getting their young children into the habit of praying, those who are lying awake at night, unwilling to turn on the lights, and those who particularly wish to express their love for Mary. One's ten fingers are enough to count the Hail Marys in the absence of the beads.

So, what is the key to the Rosary as a family devotion, said with reverence and calm, even by small children?

Make it a habit. Things get easier and more relaxed when they are habitual. It's better not to be focused on the mechanics of the Rosary, but to have them as second nature, including just having the words of the prayers slide off your tongue without any difficulty. And that takes practice. So the best way to learn is just to do!

If you are not used to praying the Rosary, or not sure how to get your children to be used to it, here is a primer.

PRIMER FOR PRAYING THE ROSARY

First, entrust the project to Mary, our Lady. Just as a child assumes his mother will make all the necessary background preparations for something important to take place, so we can be very confident in the Blessed Mother's help. A childlike attitude gets us further along to our goal.

A corollary of this confidence is the knowledge that we won't offend God with our efforts. It's important to remember this as we are stumbling along, feeling uncomfortable, and our children are perhaps behaving in a less-than-stellar manner. What makes us get frustrated is the thought that it's all so inappropriate, the antics of the children and the general failure to live up to the light-infused picture we have in our mind of our family at prayer.

But if we can remember that God is our Father, and like any father actually more tolerant, forgiving, and prone to amused enjoyment than we expect, we'll be less likely to let anger take over. Parents will definitely experience the sense of letdown when the family seems incapable of acting in a reverent, pious way. Try to remember that it will be better just to try again next time. At the minimum, you might as well laugh as you swing your beads in one hand and yank a child out from behind the sofa with the other.

You are not just aiming at some sort of success at saying prayers together today. You are aiming at instilling in your children a lifelong love of prayer. Although the normal, usual thing is for children to learn their prayers from their mother (and there are many opportunities during the day for them to practice with her), it's when their father leads the prayer that the habit of praying lasts into their adulthood.

When children become adolescents, they tend to look up to their father as the pattern of how to conduct themselves in preparation to leave the home and go out into the world. It isn't that the mother can't be an example — on the contrary, she's their first example and their

model of love. But in a way, it's just this familiarity and family-centered devotion that makes the children wonder if the rest of the world goes on in the way they have learned, and if they can trust her to provide the know-how for facing it.

When the father confirms her guidance and even raises it by initiating the things she considers important, the children are convinced.

Thus, it's vitally important that the father of the family lead the prayers, the Rosary included. You and your spouse should work together to make this happen. If you have chosen after dinner for your normal Rosary time, then obviously dinner has to be early enough to allow this to happen, particularly with young children who need to be bathed and put to bed. A particular obstacle to be overcome is the postponement of the necessary preparations for the meal, leading to the squeezing out of the Rosary time later. If Mother can work on that end of things, Father can feel calm about calling the family to the Rosary after dinner.

If the father is uncomfortable being the leader, the mother, in her wisdom and with gentle perseverance, can help him become more comfortable. She resists the urge to take over, for the sake of her family decades on, for the reasons just mentioned. She encourages him privately and lets him know how grateful she is for his leadership in so many areas, and his protection, and his bravery.

Human nature being what it is, very often "Dad leading the Rosary" boils down to Mother saying, "Honey, should we say the Rosary in a few minutes?" As we will see in chapter 9, it would be better for the father to pray on his own (in view of the family) than for the mother to be rounding everyone up, with him as one of the pack. This teaches nothing of due respect for authority, which is a branch of piety, which is what we are trying to instill! Everything in God's universe is ordered, including the family's structure, for a purpose that is greater than the parts.

In order to avoid early discouragement, begin small, as with any prayer. If the Rosary isn't already naturally a part of your life, and even if it is but the children are unused to it, begin with just the basic prayers.

As far as the prayer table goes, it's probably not going to be convenient to pray the Rosary there. Most families, in our experience, will light the candle at the prayer table and then sit in a circle (the normal gathering place of the living room is fine, but it might be prudent not to be too near the toys). Or you might light the candle in an auxiliary prayer area, such as on a mantelpiece or a sideboard. Especially at the beginning, when you are keeping it short and simple, some could kneel. Some might pace about, and some might even lie on the rug when there aren't enough seats!

Having gotten everyone gathered and ready with the candle lit, just say these prayers every evening for the first week—they correspond to the first bit of the Rosary, the "tail" that hangs down:

The Sign of the Cross
The Apostles' Creed
The Our Father (traditionally for
   the Holy Father's intentions)
Three Hail Marys (tra-
   ditionally for the virtues of faith, hope,
   and charity)
The Glory Be

The next week, you can say one decade of the Rosary (one section of ten beads). Pray the above prayers beginning at the crucifix on your beads, then announce the decade of the Rosary

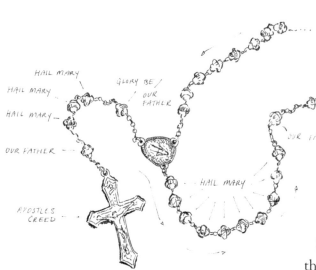

you are praying (let's say it's Monday — say, "The first Joyful Mystery, the Annunciation"), and pray one Our Father and ten Hail Marys. End with the Glory Be, make the Sign of the Cross, blow out the candle (you can let the children take turns with this), and you're done.

See how things go. As the week goes on, you will probably grow used to saying the prayers, and the decade will go more smoothly. Try not to pay attention to antics or calls for attention. Focus as much as you can on the prayers and saying them reverently. It would be good not to comment on how things went in front of the children. The important thing is that you prayed together. ·

A wonderful help for praying with children is to have cards or books with illustrations of the Mysteries of the Rosary. Some museums print postcards of their religious art, and the mysteries are subjects of some of the best Masters' paintings. There are icons as well. There are books with art for each decade. Just be sure that the art is simple and lovely, not cartoonish or infantile, because you don't want children to associate the Rosary with a stage they've outgrown, especially when it's obviously relevant to the most mature and sophisticated among us!

And of course, they would love to have their own (sturdy) rosary beads or rosary rings. You can keep these in a pretty bowl or on attractive hooks on or near the little oratory.

If things are progressing, try adding the Hail Holy Queen prayer to the end of your decade (this prayer is said at the end of the five decades of the Rosary, but we are doing the short version here). Do this for a week or more (*more* could mean years).

On the fourth week, try saying the whole Rosary — all five decades, with the first bits first (the "tail" of the beads starting with the crucifix) and the Hail Holy Queen last. If that seems too soon, change the schedule to suit your needs.

Sometimes the day isn't going to have time in it for devotions — at least not longer ones like the Rosary. But the best thing about the Rosary is how portable it is. You don't even need the beads — you have your ten fingers! Thus, it is possible to say the Rosary in the car or on a walk. Once you are familiar with it and can say the prayers without much effortful thinking, you can say it on the way to a class or to and from an event (yes, it's okay to break it up).

TRY NOT TO EXPLAIN

As you make your (undoubtedly not smooth) way to this point, keep in mind the real importance of curtailing any explaining and teaching. Those belong in non-prayer times, for the most part.

Our culture is plagued by explaining. We have lost the ability to allow experience to be the teacher, and we certainly have lost any patience for the kind of learning that comes with practice. We rely on words in a technical way, as blunt instruments for instruction. We don't rely on the meaning inherent in words of ritual, learned over time.

Parents and other teachers of the young often thwart their own purposes by constantly breaking out of a ritual in order to explain things. This interruption in itself contains a teaching—perhaps in an unintentional yet nevertheless real way. Children come to expect that prayer or ritual in general is aimed at *them*—that its only purpose is didactic; and we can see where that is going. Nowhere good.

Better to help them learn simply to experience something like communal prayer or attendance at Mass, with some brief explanations beforehand and the promise that you will answer questions afterward. Teach them to be quiet, to absorb, to listen actively. Once they learn this important habit, they will be able to attain the wonder.

Is this realistic with small children? Why yes, but you must realize that it will take a long time! Little by little, they learn. And of course, you start all over with the younger members of the family as they get older, although the effort put into training the older ones pays off here, with the younger ones naturally imitating them.

What works best is for the focus to be on the prayer (represented by the candle, and for good reason; see chapter 7), not on each other. This takes practice on the part of the participants, but with Mother and Father setting the example, the children will learn that they are not the main attraction—not even their naughtiness.

Who Prays and Who Leads Prayer in the Little Oratory?

[Fathers], your example of honesty in thought and action, joined in some common prayer, is a lesson for life, an act of worship of singular value. In this way you bring peace to your homes . . . Remember, it is thus that you build up the Church.

Pope Paul VI, General Audience,
August 11, 1976

Baptism makes living stones of God's people (see 1 Pet. 2:4–5). By Baptism we share in the priesthood of Christ, in his prophetic and royal mission, becoming "a chosen race, a royal priesthood, a holy nation, God's own people, that [we] may declare the wonderful deeds of him who called [us] out of darkness into his marvelous light" (1 Peter 2:9). "Baptism gives a share in the common priesthood of all believers" (CCC 1268).

So, to be clear, an ordained priest must celebrate Mass, but a priest is not necessary for the faithful to pray together. Of course, a priest's participation in a community Liturgy of the Hours would be of benefit to all, including to himself, but the people can pray without him and still retain the full liturgical efficacy of the prayer. This "priesthood of all believers" is a powerful force for calling on God's grace wherever we may be, for taking responsibility for our part in mediating that grace, and for being witnesses of Christ to others.

Interestingly, the Liturgy of the Hours can be prayed together liturgically even when not everyone is in communion with Rome, with the Catholic Church. In fact, a person from another congregation—even, say, a Protestant one—could *lead* the prayer! This reality makes the Divine Office an ecumenical blessing. Imagine the different congregations of a town coming together to pray Evensong together. And of course, praying the Divine Office together would be a fruitful source of unity for a married couple who belong to different communions.

And as Christians, we believe that when two or more are gathered, in some sense they are offering prayer and making present the Mystical Body of Christ for the whole of the community of believers. This knowledge gives great power and meaning to a little gathering around an icon corner in a home! Even if the family can't all be there, those who are present can pray on their behalf. If some members of the family lack commitment to family prayer, it would make no sense to force them; however, the prayers of the few can be offered for all.

WHO LEADS IN THE HOME?

"'For this reason a man shall leave his father and mother and be joined to his wife, and the two shall become one flesh.' This mystery is a profound one, and I am saying that it refers to Christ and the church; however, let each one of you love his wife as himself, and let the wife see that she respects her husband" (Eph. 5:31–33).

The woman is the heart of the home. When people stop thinking that her contribution to her family is priceless, the bottom falls out of the home. Coldness descends. The members of the family find that everywhere but home beckons to them, yet what is essential to the person, the sense of being accepted and loved for one's own sake, isn't to be found anywhere else.

"In God's eternal plan, woman is the one in whom the order of love in the created world of persons first takes root" (*Mulieris Dignitatem* 29). In the making of the little oratory in the home, as with all the aspects of making a home, the mother is often—usually—fittingly—the one who tends to oversee the details and make things homey as well as holy. This hominess is an essential part of what we look for in a home altar, because home is a foretaste of heaven; we could no more do without the specific, personal, and detailed nature of what constitutes hominess than do without the comfort and sense of belonging that we desire in the hereafter. These qualities all go together. The wise husband reveres his wife for her skillful and transcendent homemaking.

The wife and mother of the home knows how to facilitate the strength of her husband's protective care. Many today are afraid of the masculine principle of strength and power because they have only experienced either its raw force, unsoftened by any corresponding grace; or its absence, made fearful by the unknown.

But the family needs this masculine side of things in the same irreplaceable way that they need the feminine. The family needs leadership and strong example. In the Old Testament, God appoints the father to be the priest of his family, instructing them on the narrative of the covenant. He gives the blessing; he hears their responses.[4] The mother of the family encourages her husband to exhibit all the best characteristics that go along with fatherhood and leadership. She gladly allows him to lead in prayer, for instance, even if she tends to be the one who gives directives to the children.

She knows that, as the family grows, she will need the children to respect and follow her husband's example. The wise woman won't be caught off guard in later years by a husband who, having been marginalized in the day-to-day affairs of the family, finds he can't lead, or even seeks appreciation for his uniquely masculine gifts elsewhere. The wife is aware of a common error: that of forgetting that we *all* learn as we go. She doesn't make her husband bear the brunt of wifely impatience

with his own learning curve. Rather, she, being honored for her own gifts, makes room for his contribution.

A husband must be patient with his wife's attention to detail. A wife should never shame her husband with her competence, making him feel inadequate; but with her loving encouragement, he will overcome his doubts and perceived shortcomings. As Pope John Paul II notes, "in many ways [the man] has to *learn* his own '*fatherhood*' from *the mother*" (*Mulieris Dignitatem* 18). But she must do that as his loving, not scolding, wife.

Her encouragement should take the form of confidence that he is able to lead his own children. The mother needs to realize that a man has

---

4   Scott Hahn, *Letter and Spirit* (New York: Doubleday, 2005), chap. 1.

different ways of expressing himself, and his distinctively male ways (louder, deeper voice, strong or even rough movements, abrupt reactions) have value in the family. God created the man to be the way he is in order to complement the woman's softness, emotionalism, and sensitivity. And of course, her softness rounds his edges.

Together there will be a balance—a simultaneous mitigation of the excesses and enhancement of the strengths of each sex's characteristics—that benefits the whole family. The present crisis of fatherhood will be resolved only in families, where the father is allowed to regain his position of servant leader.

WHAT IF ONLY ONE PARENT PRAYS?

If only the mother prays because she is the only parent present, then her example will sustain her family spiritually. She should have recourse to St. Joseph, Jesus' foster father on earth, placing him in the position of spiritual director of her family.

If her husband is present but not willing to join in, she should take care that her prayer isn't perceived by him or by the children as a reproach.

Setting up disunity would end up being more detrimental to her goal of their spiritual and emotional maturity than if she prays in private. (In any case, children always know what their mother's disposition is, without having it explicitly displayed.) Because of the natural and scriptural headship of the husband, it might be very difficult for her to prevent being seen as forcing the children to take sides, even if that isn't her intention. If she is humble and is sure that her example isn't misunderstood, then, if she is seen to persevere in prayer, it can only help.

If only the father prays, because of his natural and scriptural headship, and provided that he too remains humble and loving toward his wife, the effect will be perceived as a powerful act of love rooted in sacrifice. Because of the father's role of leadership, what he does is seen particularly as done on behalf of the family as a whole, even if the family members don't seem to acknowledge this reality. His commitment will be a mirror of Christ's love for His Church—a willingness to die to self for her sake. There is something so evocative of humility in the sight of a man praying that his loved ones can't help being moved.

DO CHILDREN CONTRIBUTE?

"Because children have abounding vitality, because they are in spirit fierce and free, therefore they want things repeated and unchanged. They always say, 'Do it again'" (G. K. Chesterton, "The Ethics of Elfland," *Orthodoxy*).

Children have a wonderful contribution to make to the prayer life of the family. For one thing, the need to raise children properly inspires parents' growth in virtue. People have to confront all their weaknesses when there are children around! No one gets away with being too impatient or too overbearing—or too lazy to correct.

People who are used to seeing families with only one or two children always remark to parents of larger families, "You must have so much patience to have so many children!" Well, the answer is, we do acquire that virtue at some point, if we didn't have it to start with! Family life provides the struggle to acquire necessary virtues; the alternative is to consign ourselves to being miserable and making others miserable.

In general, when we parents give ourselves wholeheartedly to the task of raising children—which largely means teaching these unformed creatures self-control so that they can learn to love and grow properly —*we* learn self-control. So you can see how, although it seems daunting at first, having children at the prayer table is the best thing that can happen to the family.

Children bring something else to the prayer life of the family. They bring wonder. Life itself—even what we, sadly, consider boring—is a source of wonder to a child. A child doesn't need to be taken to a fancy theme park; a child is happy in a sandpit. Every child is predisposed to respond to *everything* with awe.

We adults have to relearn this wonder when it comes to ritual. When, in the Gospel, Jesus tells us to become like little children, what does He mean? He can't mean to be truthful or kind or strong—He has other images for those virtues, which children do not possess. No, He means us to be trusting. This is what the child teaches us: trust, with no hint of fear or even irony, leaning on God's strength as a child leans on his father.

Difficulties You May Have

We know that in everything God works
for good with those who love him, who
are called according to his purpose.

Rom. 8:28

Although we have tried to anticipate difficulties in our explanations, some may linger. Perhaps these questions and answers will help.

1. "This prayer table thing seems like a burden."

Freedom is the watchword. In this book, we are trying to present traditions in the hopes that they will attract your imagination and help your prayer life and that of your family. Of necessity, we are trying to be as complete and specific as possible. But if all this information and detail is not helping, don't feel burdened. The traditions are just ways of doing that have

the blessing of being time-tested, but they are not meant to be rules or rigid, constricting thoughts that take all your energy.

If something helps and sparks your creativity, then we've succeeded and the idea has succeeded. If not, let it go. Prayer is simply a relationship with God, who knows you and loves you, not a prescribed set of actions or ideas to check off. You can do it however you like.

2. "My whole house is very messy. I feel odd trying to have a home altar or prayer table, and I'm afraid that it will just become another messy surface. I think I need to work on organizing my life before I try this."

We encourage you to go ahead and try to clear out a space for the purpose of centralizing your spiritual "things," as well as for your prayer. You may very well experience, perhaps for the first time, how to take care of a space, and that experience may just spill over into the rest of your existence as a housekeeper. Once you commit to using a certain space in your home for a certain purpose and having it *look* a certain way—and that commitment includes *never* placing in that space anything that doesn't belong there and lovingly wiping each object down and keeping it all tidy and appealing—you will find that you suddenly understand how this sense of purpose will work for even the most mundane areas of your home.

You might think that you would need to know how to have a completely tidy house in order to be "worthy" of starting an icon corner or little oratory, but the opposite may be true. It may be that you need the discipline of taking care of what is obviously a precious area in order to understand how to care for the seemingly less-important places. (Of course, everything is important in its own way, given its own use. The whole universe has order and a rational purpose. Insofar as each thing conforms to its created purpose, it is important.)

3. "I have bad associations with the idea of an altar in the home."

This worry seems to have two manifestations on opposite ends of a spectrum. At one end,

some remember the recent past, in certain places, when the multiplication of devotions and kind people offering religious objects was rife. On the other, there is the pagan manifestation of the shrine, where the objects themselves are worshipped.

To the first thought, we simply encourage "holy housekeeping"—that is, keep only those things that are meaningful and then really *keep* them: arrange them, clean them, and have them where you can see them.

If something isn't helpful and doesn't seem even worthy of being dusted, well, then, get rid of it. Burn the palms and sprinkle the ashes in the garden rather than let them get dried out, untended, behind a picture you don't even like. Remember, these *things* are simply reminders of what is beyond. Faith is what gives them life. At the same time, a blessed object (say, a crucifix blessed by a priest) is a conveyer of the prayers of the church—it is more than itself, without being at all an object of worship. You can dispose of a blessed object that you no longer want, or that has broken, by burying it or burning it.

To the second thought, the discomfort with anything that might smack of an un-Christian magical or heathen investment of natural objects with supernatural powers, let's revert to the point that our human nature is a profound unity of the soul *and* the body. The soul is spiritual—it can't be seen or touched. The body is material.

This human nature of ours has a spiritual dimension yet won't allow us to do without any visual or material reminders at all. We can't survive without the things of this world. The error is in stopping there and investing *things* with God-like qualities. Pagans, with their shrines of statues and food offerings, incense, and flowers, commit what amounts to idolatry: offering worship to something other than God.

For the Christian, everything—including pictures of saints and even things that seem to bring a whiff of the forbidden worship in other religions, such as incense—every material thing is oriented to the worship of God alone. Offering *dulia* (reverence) or *hyperdulia* (the reverence due to our Lady) is distinct from *latria* (worship), which must be reserved for God. There is of course overlap, because human beings share the same deep desire for a connection to the past, what is above our natural life, and the afterlife. It's how we express this desire that matters!

The little oratory takes the need for a specific place and directs it in a way that's consistent with our belief in the truth of one God.

As Christians, we are aware of the danger of replacing one error—in this case, idolatry—with another, which would be iconoclasm. The Church has delved into the question and, in keeping with our human nature, which is both material and spiritual, has said this about images:

[The holy Synod commands] that images of Christ, the Virgin Mother of God, and other saints are to be held and kept especially in churches, that due honor and reverence (*debitum honorem et venerationem*) are to be paid to them, not that any divinity or power is thought to be in them for the sake of which they may be worshipped, or that anything can be asked of them, or that any trust may be put in images, as was done by the heathen who put their trust in their idols [Psalm 134:15ff], but because the honor shown to them is referred to the prototypes which they represent, so that by kissing, uncovering to, and kneeling before images we adore Christ and honor the saints whose likeness they bear. (Council of Trent, session 25)

God, "the author of beauty" (Wisd. 13:3), knows that His creatures are moved by beauty through their senses. His concern is that this movement be directed in the proper way, toward Him.

The *Catechism of the Catholic Church* has some points on the line between idolatry and the need for sensory reminders:

Nevertheless, already in the Old Testament, God ordained or permitted the making of images that pointed symbolically toward salvation by the incarnate Word: so it was with the bronze serpent, the ark of the covenant, and the cherubim.

The Christian veneration of images is not contrary to the first commandment which proscribes idols. Indeed, "the honor rendered to an image passes to its prototype," and "whoever venerates an image venerates the person portrayed in it." The honor paid to sacred images is a "respectful veneration," not the adoration due to God alone. (CCC 2130, 2132)

4. "We don't have a place for something like this."

Keep in mind that even the center of your kitchen table can be your little oratory. It's easy to find attractive wooden, metal, or composite trays or boxes at thrift or craft stores that would make a charming place on a table for a freestanding crucifix and a favorite patron saint's statue, with a little vase for flowers and a votive candle. Dinner is nicer with a little candle anyway.

The whole tray or box can be removed during meals (it can also remain on the table, of course, if there is room) and when you clean the table. The corner shelf is another space-saver. In chapter 3, you'll find details on practical aspects of the icon corner.

We really recommend that you pray for a practical solution. Often what's needed is a specific prayer, through the intercession of the Holy Family, to show you how it can be done. Then devote some critical thought to how you use the space in your home. Hopefully the illustrations in this book will spark your creativity.

5. "I don't think I have time to pray at home. I'm so busy!"

Just like anything else, you have to schedule prayer in. Maybe you aren't used to the idea of scheduling in general. Some people, for instance, eat when they are hungry. The problem is that sometimes you can get caught up in your activities and not realize that you forgot to eat! Sometimes it's too late, and you experience a meltdown or a headache—all because you don't have a schedule for eating!

When you have a family (or suffer from migraines, or both), you realize that you can't live this way. While some children will complain if they are hungry, some just quietly fade off. But you are the responsible party, and you have to make time for a meal so that being well fed isn't an issue. It just gets done.

Likewise with sleep. The physiological reality is that if we sleep only when we begin to feel sleepy, that time will come later and later each day, and of course, there are distractions that make us postpone going to bed. Soon we realize that if we don't schedule a bedtime, we'll end up short on sleep.

Prayer is the same. It's a need, really, even more so than the physical need for food and sleep. Not praying—not talking to God—would leave us worse off than starving. So we just have to schedule it in.

Make a reasonable list of priorities, starting with Mass and the precepts of the Church (discussed in chapter 5). Consider all the devotions we've discussed in this book and which ones seem to be calling out to you. Consider that the Liturgy of the Hours is liturgical prayer, and thus, even doing one Office

is corporate prayer in the sacramental life of the Church.

Once you make room for prayer, you'll find that your time opens up in a miraculous way. That happens for two reasons. First, prayer is a step out of time, into eternity. From the heavenly realm of timelessness, we are no longer slaves to the onward relentless march of earthly time.

Second, when you have put first things first, prioritizing spills over into other areas of life. (Every self-help book you will ever read comes down to this point, by the way: prioritizing. So take it a step further, into the spiritual realm.) Trying to see things the way God sees them puts everything into perspective.

Amusingly, the answer to the question of scheduling prayer and how to do it comes—in prayer! Pray about it in a specific way, by putting the issue of your priorities before God, and then think it over. The answer will come. As with everything else, keep it simple. Whatever you choose will be pleasing to God, who only wants to be near you.

You'll find that trying to fit a liturgical pattern into your day gives way to fitting your day into the liturgical pattern. Since the latter is God's way, it stands to reason that there is more order in it and that it gives us more control over our life.

You can find the symbolism of living in harmony with God's priorities for your time in holy icons. In an icon, we see an image of a saint, for instance. This saint is a wise and holy person who doesn't act rashly, but is open to inspiration — either directly from God or mediated through the material world. The saint thinks before he acts, and he acts wisely.

In the icon, the face of a saint is painted to symbolize this reality. Those organs that receive information are enlarged. The nose, which takes in the fragrance of the heavenly breath, is slightly elongated. The ears (unless hidden by hair or cloth) are proportionately larger than expected.

The organs that involve action, on the other hand, are proportionately reduced. When they act, saints act decisively and effectively but with economy of effort. The saint's mouth is small — no gossip or mindless chatter escapes it — but when he speaks, every word is golden.

The slim and graceful hands and fingers rest in a gentle gesture, lacking in calluses if the saint is a working one, like St. Joseph. No efforts are wasted, although he works hard.

Even implementing a small plan of prayer will yield great results in "holy time management." Distraction will be less; interest will be greater; life as a whole will be better directed. Take small steps to reap great rewards.

6. "I can't find nice things to make a little oratory."

It's true that beautiful objects can be hard to find. In the section on making your prayer table (chapter 3), we've given you some ideas on how to go about it. Mainly, you'll find that becoming acquainted with thrift stores and even junk shops can help with finding what you need, because older things tend to be of better quality. However, you must train your eye, because many older things are just as tacky as new ones. Really *look* at the object to see if it has the qualities that make it worth having — qualities of line, form, manufacture, color, weight, and size.

Although it is best to have original artwork, reproductions are fine if you can't afford or find original art — provided they are done well. Just be aware that when art is very well known, it tends to disappear. By that, we mean that one hardly sees it when one looks at it. All that registers is the fact of the representation and possibly the name of the artist ("Right, Leonardo da Vinci's *Last Supper*"). It's hard to *look* at that art and take in what it is meant to depict. (Ironically, it also devalues the work to have it reproduced so widely. It happens that when you finally have the chance to see the *Pietà* at St. Peter's, you may hardly be able to take it in because it's so familiar to you.) However, it is better to have a good reproduction of the right painting, than a substandard original. If you are going to use a reproduction (and, to be honest, most of us are), take the time to mount and frame it attractively.

We've noticed that there are more artists who are meeting the demand for good affordable art, and in the resources we try to point you in the right direction. If you come across an artist whose work you admire, encourage him by buying his art for your home. And, of course, there are the icons included in this book to help you get started.

7. *"I would like to try, but my children are heedless. It won't last."*

Well, it's precisely by experiencing the wonder of something precious that children learn to be mindful and gentle, treating precious things with respect. Children are not animals, but they can act like animals if no one ever requires any other behavior from them. Yet, when they encounter something awe-worthy, they respond very well.

Lighting a candle, having a spot where you gather, allowing a moment to appreciate the wonder of addressing the good God, and, paradoxically, turning your attention away from the children toward something beyond—these help. Build up the practice of these things gradually.

Involve children in the care of the little oratory and show them its uses and how to handle the objects. It's when we, the adults, are haphazard about caring for things that our children blunder about; their attention is understandably elsewhere. They like to be shown exactly what to do, and they like having the right materials with which to do it. Children as young as two or three can learn

the steps of dusting, wiping, changing vase water, preparing stems of flowers, discarding spent blooms, properly disposing of matches, and so forth, as described in chapter 3.

If you yourself think through each of these steps, providing the necessary items (dust cloths in a special container, metal dish for matches), you might find that your children will soon become more fastidious than you expected (or perhaps more fastidious than you are!).

Discovering the need for mindfulness in the little oratory alerts us to the larger need to be mindful in general—to become aware of having consideration for other people and for things. The things we do in the home, including prayer at the little oratory, facilitate the process of growing in awareness of the world around us. Now we are back to the home as school of virtue!

8. "I tried what you said about praying together, but my children won't sit or stand still."

Well, they are either very young or unused to prayerful, quiet behavior, or both.

These things take time and practice. Even a small child can sit still for the first bit of whatever devotion it is you are doing, especially if you ask with firmness. Before you start, tell the children that you expect them to stay with you for that part, and then, when you give them the nod, they can choose to stay put or go off to play quietly (you can designate appropriate activities beforehand if you don't want them chasing each other with toy machine guns during your evening prayer). Set your expectations low, but do make your expectations clear.

Be patient, gently remind your children of the posture you expect, eject those who are too squirmy, and begin again.

9. "They still misbehave."

Stop focusing on them. That's not easy or always possible, but it pays to try. Notice your own posture and the direction of your gaze when you pray. Very often, parents tend to look intently at their children while they pray. Yet, one of the most important things they can do is to look away, toward an icon or a crucifix or a candle. This lets their children know that they are not the center of attention. Soon, if you are consistent, they will become aware of another presence and a holy atmosphere.

Indeed, make it a practice to pray there without reference to the child. Simply pause briefly for your own moment of prayer and then move on. Little by little the children will imitate you—*if* you let go of any need for them to do so.

In order to attain the awareness of a holy atmosphere, of course, children must be able to behave. So it's a bit of a paradox. Just as in other instances of naughtiness that pop up in your day, you will have to stop what you are doing (you or your spouse, while the other continues the prayer) and put a stop to bad behavior in whatever way seems appropriate—maybe just taking the child off for his bedtime routine, maybe sitting him apart from the others for the duration. If the prayer goes on without him, he will learn that it's worth it not to misbehave. Remember at the end of the prayer to share some relaxed moments together, at the minimum, rather than abruptly finishing and parting. Enjoying each other's company after prayer, chatting, laughing, and sharing news, makes for truly lovely family time. Even if people have to scatter, it's worthwhile to make it a goal to have a few moments, at least, of togetherness. This enjoyable visiting time becomes something to look forward to, once the child experiences it. It will be an incentive not to have to leave because of bad behavior.

Please know that if you persevere, even though it seems impossible, you will arrive at a time when your family will behave very nicely at prayer and everywhere else. It's a matter of putting in the effort, being patient, and waiting. Really.

10. "Where we live, there are no flowers."

Here is where you may start your education in beauty! Can you see beauty in the weeds, in low-hanging branches of bushes and trees, in grasses, and in wildflowers? Even in the city, you can go for a walk. We have to see the beauty that is around us. If our preconceived ideas of formally arranged roses with baby's breath blind us, then what hope is there? The humble stalk of a wild aster growing by the road will be lovelier on your prayer table than an expensive arrangement. Our advice is to let your children find the flowers.

11. "The Liturgy of the Hours seems like a lot of work."

Here are some tips for incorporating the Liturgy of the Hours or some aspect of them into your life without a lot of work. Again, this is all simply for your edification. If it is burdensome, don't worry at all. You have complete freedom. Remember that prayer is simply conversation with God.

Most people begin their Divine Office journey by doing one or two Offices each day. The morning and evening Offices of Lauds and Vespers are the most important and are sometimes referred to as the hinges on which the whole Divine Office turns. Compline, the

night Office, is short, and because it can be said just before we go to bed, it is often easier to fit into a busy routine. You can memorize it pretty easily. You might find that your children memorize it before you do!

Don't worry if you forget or are too busy even to do this. Just keep trying. If your experience is like ours, your life will gradually start to conform to the pattern of your prayer and you will find it easier to make time.

Only when this first target is a comfortable part of your daily routine should you think about doing more. You might try one of the little Hours during the day. Perhaps you are able to get up a little earlier in the morning and pray the Office of Readings. One of the Offices may be the one prayer that spouses have a chance to share during a busy day, so they make it a priority.

It might be helpful to simplify the Offices. This practice is not an innovation. Even in St. Benedict's Rule we can find the psalms for the traditional Offices of Terce, Sext, and None remaining unchanged (in the Paul VI psalter they are called the Complementary Psalms for Prayer during the Day). Also, it is a long-standing tradition to sing the same Compline every day using the second Sunday Compline.

In the appendix "Patterns in the Church's Liturgy," you will find a discussion of the significance of the pattern of seven plus one—the Old Testament covenantal number of seven, plus the one of Jesus, yielding the Eighth Day of heavenly approach. The Liturgy of the Hours follows this pattern by marking the seven plus one (the Mass) "Hours" of the day.

This pattern can help us choose a simple yet liturgically connected prayer method. Here are a few different ideas that might help. The point is to do something calm and above all, *possible* for our particular circumstances.

Instead of adding Hours from the Office, pray a psalm or part of one, such as an antiphon (perhaps the Communion antiphon from the day's Mass), for instance, at midday. You can memorize Psalm 117, which is just four lines long, to pray at one of the times for a Liturgical Hour if you are unable to say the whole thing.

Try a pocket New Testament and Psalms. Each day, read a psalm to mark an Hour. For Lauds, Vespers, and Compline, read the appropriate Gospel canticle. For Lauds, it's the Canticle of Zechariah (Luke 1:68–79, also called the Benedictus); for Vespers, the Canticle of Mary (Luke 1:46–55, also called the Magnificat); and for Compline, the Canticle of Simeon (Luke 2:29–32, also called the Nunc Dimittis).

These canticles are printed at the back of every issue of *Magnificat* magazine. You could simply tear them out of an old one and carry them about.

Of course, even a simple Our Father, Hail Mary, and Glory Be would be appropriate for marking the Hours. The *Catechism* reminds us that the Jesus Prayer (discussed in the appendices) is very powerful and ordered to the Liturgy. Many devotional prayers, such as the Angelus and the Rosary, developed as ways of marking the liturgical pattern of daily prayer.

The target is to try to establish a routine of coming back to God eight times in each twenty-four hours of the day. Once this pattern of prayer is established using very simple and quick prayers in any situation, it will become easier (gradually!) to pray a full Office for the Hour (most of which take only ten minutes to pray).

THE WELL BALANCED SPIRITUAL LIFE

A well balanced spiritual life contains the Liturgy, non-liturgical devotions, Scripture reading, and mental prayer, as well as good works. Each person is unique. Advice from a spiritual director on achieving a liberating balance, taking into account our whole life situation, is a good idea. If at any point trying to do any of this seems a burden or a source of anxiety, or if it seems too complicated after giving it a reasonable attempt, then it is almost certain that we have taken on too much.

Remember, as laypeople with lots of other duties, we may not ever be able to go further in adding prayers and devotions. But quantity isn't the measure of holiness; rather, it's our relationship with God that matters.

You needn't continually seek novel ways of praying as an indication of progress. Once you reach a balance that is right for you—that is, the one that God intends for you—just keep on doing it. Be happy in knowing that, by God's grace, you're going forward on the pilgrimage to heaven. The power to move forward comes from your willingness to co-operate with God's grace to be transformed supernaturally.

Transform the Home, Transform the World

*For he has made known to us in all wisdom
and insight the mystery of his will, according
to his purpose which he set forth in Christ as a
plan for the fulness of time, to unite all things
in him, things in heaven and things on earth.*

Eph. 1:9–10

W hen we live the Faith, we change things.

Maybe you've had the experience of being in a group of strangers who take turns telling a bit about themselves. Each person will likely express himself in terms of the relationships he has with others and the places he belongs to. Each wants to be known as a father, a mother, a friend of someone else in the room, a member of a company or a university. Even if a person describes himself only as a chemist, he will say where he is from.

We naturally express ourselves in terms of relationship. The human person, starting right from birth, is defined by his relationship to his mother and his father, and this is necessary to us for our happiness. No one can be happy apart from the matrix of connections he has with others—with society. We often fall into the error of thinking of the human being as an individual—someone who can live autonomously, taking or leaving his connections with others, a unit like other units, replaceable. In fact, a human being is a *person*—someone unique, with a rational soul, with irreplaceable bonds he forms with other persons in relationships.

God came to live among us as one of us, also being born in a family and growing in a particular place, in order to make evident to us the importance, not only of these human relationships, but of the divine relationship which is the Trinity—three Persons in a relationship in the one Godhead.

The love between persons (whether human or divine) itself has existence. Something new and real is created between two or more when there is love. This "something" is the willing of the good for the other—the manifestation of the Golden Rule, which is to treat others as another self, wanting for them what we want for ourselves, which is the very best.

And love does not have to mean only what we

normally attribute to the word. Any relationship, however casual, can (and should) incorporate the motive of desiring the good of the other. Even a cheery hello to a shopkeeper can reflect a loving motive for the good.

THROUGH OUR PERSONAL RELATIONSHIPS WE CAN CHANGE THE WORLD

God so loved the world that He gave His only Son. This Son was born among us, the Word made flesh, taught us, was crucified, and rose again. He left his "being among us" in the Eucharist, the Sacred Liturgy, which daily gives us the Word, Jesus. It's not something in the past. It is in the now, and we take part in it as surely as we take part in all our relationships—a give-and-take of love! This understanding of the human person and his relationships with others and with God has a profound effect on how we view what society is. It is not a collective of self-contained individuals, but a beautiful edifice made by all the interactions of love between each person within that society. And most of all, what is done in the home and in the Church will be what is brought into society as a whole.

It's not enough to have something beautiful and meaningful in the family, in the home. It's not enough to have something beautiful and profound in the Church. There must be a connection between the two, so that the person who is nourished, body and soul, in each place, can bring grace out into the world.

We believe that something as little as a prayer table or icon corner — of course, meaning what is done there, which is all the things covered in this book and more — can be that connection. We think that the personal transformation in Christ that happens in the Sacred Liturgy can be communicated through the persons in the family and through the days of the week, in every activity and interaction. This communication — the Word — then gets carried out where it is most needed, to all the communities of which we are a part.

It's not that we will do anything different in an outward way. It's just that, having centered ourselves in Christ, we will be taking Him wherever we go. This orientation works with our personality and has nothing to do with any outward show of piety or a holier-than-thou attitude. No, the change comes simply from beginning to be more united with Christ.

The more direct our personal connection is with people and communities, the more profound the effect. Through the network of personal relationships, one person can touch the world. The most straightforward way is to pray directly for every connection we can think of.

At Church during the Mass and at home in the little oratory we pray *for* others, but we also pray on behalf of others.

We pray for family members near and far, our work, and our country. We pray for those in our family who have passed away, for the forgotten souls, and for those yet to be born.

But we pray *for* others in another sense. We pray for them when they do not pray for themselves, acting with the priesthood of our Baptism to offer for them a pleasing sacrifice to God. This is so even when we pray alone — when no one else knows of our participation. Sometimes others can't be with us at the moment to join in prayer. Sometimes they won't. Regardless, we can join our prayers to those of the Eternal Priest and the whole Church on their behalf.

THE SACRED LITURGY IS THE PRAYER THAT CREATES AND BINDS COMMUNITIES

The faith lived in our homes, perhaps enlivened in the little oratory, can therefore be a real force for good in society. This is true of any prayer that we make together (or on our own), but particularly powerfully of the Liturgy of the Hours, which, as we have seen, is the prayer of the whole Church. Family, friends, parish, the whole universal Church, workplace, town, country — will all benefit from our participation in the Liturgy, the life of Christ.

WHAT ABOUT AT WORK?

Culture is a word that reflects the cult that is at the core of it — that is to say, the worship (*cultus* in Latin). What arises from worship is what becomes the culture. This whole book has been one vast effort to make the cult at the heart of the home beautiful and true and good, enough so as to give rise to a worthy culture for the family and the world beyond.

But what of doing the same in other settings? Given this truth, that the culture arises from worship, it is no surprise that businesses in our society, which typically give no thought to liturgical piety at all, reflect a secular culture. For it is true that having *no* worship at the center will *not* give rise to nothing. The vacuum will be filled with the default form of worship; perhaps that will be the worship of money, or power, or just distraction.

It's interesting to note that most managed organizational change in the workplace will be temporary or superficial, because rarely does it really do anything to change the culture, which is a product of how people interact naturally based on what is important to them. To change a culture, you must change the cult; to change something as particular as an organization, you must change what it rests on — what is important to it — what it "worships," so to speak.

Even those of us who are used to the idea that the place for right worship is in church and the home would overlook the workplace or consider it appropriate for silent and invisible prayer only. Maybe we would confine ourselves to an occasional prayer for help! Maybe the assumption is that the workplace simply competes with family and church for our time and energy. Can the workplace aspire to be a community of love?

Here are some thoughts. First, you can make the most discreet of little oratories at your desk. Most people have photos of their family around their work area — little snaps of the kids with their soccer balls or dance shoes, a wedding photo. Arrange things so that centered among these, on the wall above your computer screen or on the corner of your desk, is a crucifix icon, such as the San Damiano crucifix of St. Francis, which can be obtained in a small size, or a little pewter crucifix. If you have room, put a few prayer cards on either side — our Lady and a patron saint. St. Joseph, patron of workers, is a good choice.

The whole thing can take up less than eight inches and be quite unobtrusive. If someone

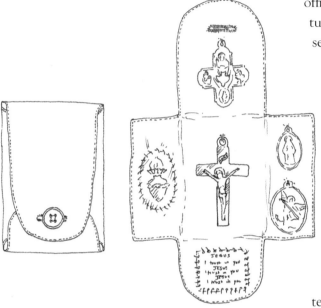

brings you flowers on your birthday, one of the posies can go in a little vase before the picture of Mary. But a crucifix alone is enough—all of three inches!

If you are at work, you can make a point of praying the Office for your colleagues. Everyone needs a break during work, and the Hours provide the perfect rest, taking up less than ten minutes for the most part. No need to make any show. Simply take out your Breviary or *Magnificat*, or open Universalis.com on your device, nod imperceptibly to the crucifix, and pray silently. Have no doubt that even this hidden witness works toward creating a community of love in the midst of the most sterile office environment. This will be a true cultural change, even though you may not see the effects.

If, in natural conversation with your coworkers, you find that anyone shows interest—and if practicalities allow (sometimes they will not)—let them know when you pray the Liturgy of the Hours and invite them to join you. Then you would be invoking the public aspect of Liturgy. In some places, such as a college, it might be possible to extend an invitation to the general public to attend the community prayer, which would create a wider scope. But even if you never do anything other than pray silently on your own (with the whole heavenly host, of course), you will be doing your part to share your relationship with God with your companions.

Harmony with heaven is harmony with the family and with the world. This life of prayer in our communities will tend toward the common good. To the degree that it does, it supports and enriches every other element of goodwill. The sense of conflict between persons and within persons can diminish. Instead of feeling pulled apart by the internal needs of work, rest, and family life, we will find peace. Disparate goals will retain their differences but become complementary components of one unified life.

FAMILY HOSPITALITY

When the rhythm of prayer becomes natural in the family, it can easily involve guests. Although we can feel slightly embarrassed, the fact is that most people are wide open to entering into the normal routines of the family, truly enjoy helping and participating, and are very interested in prayer traditions. Welcoming others for a meal and family Vespers or dessert and Compline can be a lovely and meaningful occasion. Of course, we need to be sensitive to the expectations of the people whom we invite, and sometimes it's not appropriate or, for some reason, wouldn't strike them as natural behavior, even if it is natural to us! And of course, skipping prayer for the sake of hospitality is no failing, but simply the exercise of charity.

Sometimes a powerful example might be for the father to explain that he prays on behalf of the family, and to excuse himself for fifteen minutes, inviting anyone who wishes to join him.

There are various ways to handle guests and their inclusion in the prayer life of the family. In chapter 2 we spoke of an indefinable sense of presence that a person experiences when he enters your home. The home centered on prayer is very healing to others. We encourage you to be confident in inviting people to your family life of prayer.

We especially encourage you to invite your parish priests to supper to bless your family oratory. Your family will get to know your priests, and they will get to know you.

THE LITURGY OF THE HOURS IN THE LIFE OF THE PARISH

The natural community of the Church is the parish. To be grounded, folks need to live in the place where they are, which sounds tautological until you reflect on the propensity we all have of jumping into the car to go elsewhere. The parish is the geographical location—the place—that brings the faithful together for worship. Healing of divided communities, especially divided spiritual communities, will take place through the parish. The parish is where you get married, where your children are baptized, and where your loved ones are buried. It's where you have a priest who knows you and where you come from. It's in your neighborhood—even if you live somewhere that doesn't seem to have one.

Even for those who have moved, a parish supplies the sense of belonging. The past forty years have seen a terrible evisceration of the parish, especially among the most committed Catholics, some of whom have fled to escape liturgical abuses. All of this is understandable, and "shopping for a parish" has become commonplace. Yet, the geographical parish must be nurtured back to wholeness.

The little oratory can be part of the prescription for the long-term revival of the parish. In the home, living the faith in the liturgical year, with simple participation in the Liturgy of the Hours and traditional devotions, the family grows. In the parish, the priest ministers through the sacraments and prays his Breviary in his normal priestly life.

It used to be, in some parishes, that the people prayed Vespers together with their priest. Maybe today, with families learning to pray Vespers on their own, say, during Advent, the thought might arise to pray together, as a parish with their priest, thereby renewing this aspect of parish life that has been all but lost.

Perhaps you have a music director who is adept at helping the people to chant (see some easy thoughts on this in the appendices), which isn't very difficult, once you get the hang of it. Perhaps a few families have begun meeting together at their home altars to pray together occasionally.

Little by little, these families begin asking their priest for a bit more. This affirms him rather than burdening him, for what does he live for other than to serve his parishioners? At the same time, they see the work that's heaped on his head in the running of the church and put their skills at his service. Your authors do not want you to oppress your pastor! But we do want to encourage you to ask for more in the spiritual sense.

In particular, praying an Office in the parish church — meeting for Lauds on the way to school, for instance; or singing Vespers for a feast day such as the Immaculate Conception — does two things for the life of the parish in its people and its priest. First, because the Office extends the Mass, it enables the people and their priest to linger over moments that go by all too quickly, especially when the priest is managing multiple Masses or the people are managing multiple children. At Vespers, often the Gospel of the day is offered for further pondering. We have a chance in the antiphon to linger over it. If Benediction is offered as well, the moment of Consecration is enlarged for us. If we've gone to Mass in the morning, Vespers is a way to bring the connection with the Mass back into the evening. Sharing that reality with the priest and the others of the parish expands it in our life.

Second, praying an Office with the priest gives all — himself and the people — a different perspective on his priesthood. Unlike the Mass, anyone can pray the Liturgy of the Hours even without the priest; thus, he has a different role.

At Vespers, for instance, the choir, rather than the priest, can lead the antiphons. The priest may read the short reading and even offer a reflection. But it's not like his central role at Mass.

In a way, you might say that celebrating the Liturgy of the Hours together may restore an element integral to worship that was lost when the priest turned to face the people — namely, the sense of offering prayer and worship *with* his people *toward* God. Too often, the priest is seen (and perhaps sees himself) as a sort of master of ceremonies, an entertainer almost. This is an unfortunate consequence of some misunderstandings of the reform of the Liturgy that came out of Vatican II.

HELPING OUR PRIESTS

In order to reform the reform, the priest and his people must be re-formed. They must see things differently, but perhaps the only way to bring this about is to *do* differently. Habits are so deeply entrenched at Sunday Mass that it's salutary to come together in a ritual prayer that is *not* the Mass. The priest recovers his vocation as true servant-leader when the parish recovers the fullness of the Liturgy.

This experience of praying the Liturgy of the Hours with the parish enriches the priest's understanding of his consecrated priesthood — his indispensability to his people when celebrating the sacraments. He recovers the sense of acting in the person of Christ — wrests it from the grip of a deadening entertainment or theater model. The people's baptismal priesthood reorients his consecrated priesthood.

All this can be accomplished, again, by means of the little oratory of the home. And this is because when a family has set up their little home altar or icon corner, they naturally invite the priest over for supper to bless it and pray with them. When he makes friends with them and sees them trying to live their Faith at home, he's greatly heartened in his mission. His bond with them as his people strengthens. He gets to know the families that make up his flock. In turn, they see his challenges and hear his concerns. They stop thinking of him as a distant figure and come to know him well. When two or three fathers of families, or the music director with a few choir members (who happen also to be families with prayer corners) approach him, asking him to see if he would be open to a Vespers service for a holy day, he will certainly be enthusiastic about sharing this part of his own devotions with them.

Vespers on Sundays and on Feasts especially are a very good thing in the parish. *Sacrosanctum Concilium* encourages us: "Pastors of souls should see to it that the chief hours, especially Vespers, are celebrated in common in church on Sundays and the more solemn feasts. And the laity, too, are encouraged to recite the divine office, either with the priests, or among themselves, or even individually" (100). And it says: "It is, moreover, fitting that the office, both in choir and in common, be sung when possible" (99).

THE CULTURE GROWS

We would also like to propose the idea of Vespers on a day that is *not* a Sunday, in order to encourage the thought that religion is not confined to one day a week. In some places in the early part of the twentieth century in America, weekly Vespers were an occasion for young people to go out to church and socialize a bit afterward—say, on a Wednesday evening. Those were harder times, but it may be that, after all, we need to recover the notion of what to do in hard times.

Some might scoff at the thought of today's young people being interested in such a thing, but those scoffers might be surprised. If the service were kept simple and beautiful (and reasonably short), with chant or traditional polyphony, which appeals to every age and taste as something other than what anyone normally encounters, it would be considered a normal part of the church experience.

Afterward, a simple potluck or soup supper in the parish hall with something like what the Irish call a *ceilidh* (pronounced, counterintuitively, "kaylee")—a casual party with folk music provided by the guests, traditional dancing, and storytelling. This type of gathering offers families (as well as those who need to be near families) a warm social event. People can reach back to any of the wonderful traditions they may remember or see celebrated in their own ethnic heritage, or they can make up their own, depending on the talents represented among them. This type of gathering was how the families of the past kept their older children enjoying social occasions under their watchful eye. At the same time, it gives kids a lot of freedom to be with their friends.

The little oratory indeed contributes to the building of the culture. It's hard to imagine, in our society today, a need greater than this, of ways for the family to pray together with others in their parish and to enjoy each other's company along with their priests. When young people are raised this way, they have an integrated way of looking at life and the choices that are before them.

12

Go Forth!

We mentioned in the introduction how often we ourselves yearned for a way to pray and live our life, spiritual and otherwise, in a unified, coherent way. We came to realize that we needed *liturgical* prayer — that is to say, prayer with the mind of the Church.

The little oratory offers that and more. It connects the family's life of faith with the parish's, which, of course, is the universal Church's. And then the life of evangelism — of the beggar telling the other beggar where to find bread — comes alive, because it's not our own idea (which may be so sadly misguided), but the idea of Christ Himself, reaching out to others through us. This is what it means to be Eucharistic, to love with the heart of the Church. For us, it was a relief to discover that we had an operating method for decision making when it comes to which devotions, which prayers, which Scriptures, which theological insights to emphasize and choose. We ourselves are not up to the task of sorting through all the options, and we don't

like the feeling that in choosing one thing, we are perhaps ignoring others that are equally important or even more important.

The life of the Church preserves us from this sad fate. Put your boat in that river, and you are bound to go somewhere good. That conviction is why, above all, we want you to receive this book in the spirit with which it's offered: that of freedom and close adherence to God's plan in the Liturgy.

Your step should be light, your heart easy. We aren't burdening you with yet

another heavy load. The most important part of our message, which we hope we've conveyed, is the *ordering principle*—not any particular quantity of observance—that allows you to select the beautiful pattern of prayer that is perfect for you and your family, offered by Christ Himself.

We want to emphasize the message of every authority from our Lord down to Pope Francis: the important thing is to *pray*, not to "say prayers." Prayer is a conversation with God; sometimes it's even a silent conversation, like the best times we have with our dearest friends—just being together and enjoying each other's company.

The paradox is that the Liturgy, with its strong structure, frees us to do just that—yet, this fact seems to be unknown to many, including many of the most devoted souls with their clever ideas for our spiritual advancement.

Whenever you are unsure about something relating to the spiritual life—especially something that seems so helpful to others—we encourage you to ask, "Does this bring me closer to Jesus, the center of my life? That is, does it bring me closer to His Liturgy? To Him in the Eucharist? To His Word? Will it make things more difficult? Will I feel guilty and waste energy on managing that feeling, rather than simply drawing nearer to Him?"

The final question is to inquire whether the pattern of prayer we choose enlivens our conviction that, above all, this nourishment must be shared with others. To bring Christ to others, to desire the good for them, to wish fellowship with Him for them—this is the proof of the rightness of the path.

The way you answer, within yourself, all these questions will give you the key to the nourishment of your prayer life. We leave it up to you. We ourselves are on the journey.

May we meet you at the final heavenly destination.

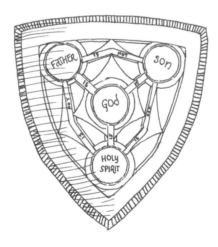

Appendices

Appendix A

—————— ❧ ——————

Devotion to Mary (and the Saints)

the Relationship between the Rosary and the Liturgy

Devotion to the saints is inseparable from the Faith. The doctrine of the Communion of Saints assures us of our interconnectedness. Simply put, we friends of Jesus Christ take care of each other and pray for each other. That "cloud of witnesses" which goes before us is assuredly deeply interested in our welfare.

Outside the Liturgy, where the saints are feasted and honored, there are many traditions of piety we can draw on. If, for example, St. Joseph is a favorite (as well he should be), we can speak to him in the fellowship of prayer very naturally.

Since Mary has a special place in the heart of the Church, we can apply any discussion of devotion to her to articulate some general principles that apply the saints in general as well.

The *Catechism* explains everything very clearly.

"All generations will call me Blessed": The Church's devotion to the Blessed Virgin is intrinsic to Christian worship. The Church rightly honors the Blessed Virgin with special devotion. From the most ancient times the Blessed Virgin has been honored with the title of "Mother of God," to whose protection the faithful fly in all their dangers and needs. This very special devotion differs essentially from the adoration which is given to the incarnate Word and equally to the Father and the Holy Spirit, and greatly fosters this adoration.

The liturgical feasts dedicated to the Mother of God and Marian prayer, such as the rosary, an "epitome of the whole Gospel," express this devotion to the Virgin Mary. (CCC 971)

The place of Mary in the Liturgy, just as in life, is privileged. Every day at Vespers we sing the Canticle of Mary, the Magnificat. After Compline every night it is customary to sing one of the Marian anthems, such as the Regina Caeli. In addition to the Marian feasts in the calendar, there is the option to commemorate her every Saturday in the Liturgy, provided that there isn't another obligatory commemoration. The Universalis website tells us:

> The memorial is a remembrance of the maternal example and discipleship of the Blessed Virgin Mary who, strengthened by faith and hope, on that great Saturday on which Our Lord lay in the tomb, was the only one of the disciples to hold vigil in expectation of the Lord's resurrection; it is a prelude and introduction to the celebration of Sunday, the weekly memorial of the Resurrection of Christ; and it is a sign that the "Virgin Mary is continuously present and operative in the life of the Church."

The antiphon for the very first psalm of an ordinary Saturday[5] tells us why we venerate her

and how she directs us to God: *Christ is the Son of Mary; come let us adore Him.*

THE ROSARY (AND THE ANGELUS)

The Rosary has a special place in devotion to Mary. So many popes and great saints over the years have recommended it. In the Rosary, we consider the life of our Lord in the Mysteries. The Rosary's very structure echoes of the structure of the Divine Liturgy: the 150 Hail Marys of the original form represented the 150 psalms said in the Liturgy of the Hours. The Angelus, in the way that it marks three Hours (morning, noon, and evening) is derived from and points to the Liturgy. However, neither prayer is liturgical; thus, we always accord higher status to the Sacred Liturgy, the Mass, and to the Liturgy of the Hours, the prayer of the Universal Church.

Praying the Rosary, although highly recommended, is not essential to a devotion to the Blessed Virgin. There are and have been many devout Catholics who also have a deep and genuine love of the Mother of God—among them, many Eastern Rite Catholics—whose devotion takes other forms.

For further reading on the subject, see Paul VI's *For the Right Ordering and Development of Devotion to the Blessed Virgin Mary.*

Some other thoughts on the Rosary and devotion to Our Lady:

---

[5] In the UK version of the Paul VI psalter.

Paul VI, *Marialis Cultus*: 48. Once the pre-eminent value of liturgical rites has been reaffirmed it will not be difficult to appreciate the fact that the Rosary is a practice of piety which easily harmonizes with the liturgy. The Rosary is an exercise of piety that draws its motivating force from the liturgy and leads naturally back to it, if practiced in conformity with its original inspiration. It does not, however, become part of the liturgy. In fact, meditation on the mysteries of the Rosary, by familiarizing the hearts and minds of the faithful with the mysteries of Christ, can be an excellent preparation for the creation of those same mysteries in the liturgical action and can also become a continuing echo thereof. However, it is a mistake to recite the Rosary during the celebration of the liturgy …

54. But there is no doubt that, after the celebration of the Liturgy of the Hours, the high point which family prayer can reach, the Rosary should be considered as one of the best and most efficacious prayers in common that the Christian family is invited to recite.

John Paul II, *Rosarium Virginis Mariae* (On the Most Holy Rosary): 13. The Rosary, in its own particular way, is part of this varied panorama of "ceaseless" prayer. If the Liturgy, as the activity of Christ and the Church, is a saving action par excellence, the Rosary too, as a "meditation" with Mary on Christ, is a salutary contemplation. By immersing us in the mysteries of the Redeemer's life, it ensures that what he has done and what the Liturgy makes present is profoundly assimilated and shapes our existence.

43. Rediscover the Rosary in the light of Scripture, in harmony with the Liturgy, and in the context of your daily lives.

From the *Directory of Popular Piety and the Liturgy*: 200. [T]he liturgical character of a given day takes precedence over the usual assignment of a mystery of the Rosary to a given day; the Rosary is such that, on particular days, it can appropriately substitute meditation on a mystery so as to harmonize this pious practice with the liturgical season.

Pope Benedict XVI's address at the Basilica of Saint Mary Major, Saturday, May 3, 2008 on the Rosary: When reciting the Rosary, the important and meaningful moments of salvation history are relived. The various steps of Christ's mission are traced. With Mary the heart is oriented toward the mystery of Jesus. Christ is put at the center of our life, of our time, of our city, through the contemplation and meditation of his holy mysteries of joy, light, sorrow and glory. May Mary help us to welcome within ourselves the grace emanating from these mysteries, so that through us we can "water" society, beginning with our daily relationships, and purifying them from so many negative forces, thus opening them to the newness of God.

HOW SHOULD YOU *FEEL* ABOUT MARY AND THE SAINTS?

It may be that you're not very attracted to Marian devotion or literature at the moment. Some people are less sentimental by nature, and some devotionals are *very* sentimental by nature. It's not surprising that some people simply don't resonate with that type of thing. For some men, particularly, there's a sense that there may be something less than masculine about certain expressions of honor to the Blessed Virgin. Many people are uncomfortable with what they perceive as undue reverence for a human being, as if some sort of idolatry is being perpetrated.

This can be a barrier for those who are otherwise drawn to traditional practices of the Faith. What can help is to read the *Catechism* on the subject, to study Scripture with an open mind, and to notice that the Church Fathers, Eastern Christians, and Church Councils don't define devotion in any strictly emotional way.

Love and reverence for Mary can be expressed in different ways. Open the Breviary to the Office of Readings for a Saturday memorial to the Blessed Virgin. You will find excerpts from sermons and writings of St. Proclus and St. John Chrysostom (both early archbishops of Constantinople), the Constitution of the Second Vatican Council, and Blessed Abbot Guerric, a Cistercian from twelfth-century France. Their clear explanations of what is good, right, and fitting will bring peace and edification on the question of these devotions.

Appendix B

The Jesus Prayer

The name 'Jesus' contains all: God and man and the whole economy of salvation ... His name is the only one that contains the presence it signifies" (CCC 2666).

The Jesus prayer is most commonly associated with the Eastern Church and is simply as follows: *Lord Jesus Christ, Son of God, have mercy on me a sinner*. Since it is so deeply traditional, and so many from both East and West find it a fruitful gateway to contemplation, we touch on two ways to incorporate it into your life of prayer.

A SUBSTITUTE FOR THE OFFICE

First, to mark a liturgical Hour (for instance, if we can't pray the whole Office associated with that Hour for some reason) with the following short set of prayers, which can easily be memorized. This takes about a minute to pray.

O God, come to my aid;
O Lord make haste to help me.

Glory be to the Father and to the Son and to the Holy Spirit. As it was in the beginning is now and ever shall be, world without end, Amen.

Lord Jesus Christ, Son of God, have mercy on me a sinner (eight times).

Kyrie eleison,
Christe eleison,
Kyrie eleison.

Our Father ...

O God, be in our thoughts and words and deeds. Send Your Holy Spirit to guide us that we may complete Your will, grace responding to grace. May the beauty of our work inspire those who see it to love as Christ loved, that through our praise of You and charity to others all may know peace and joy, through Jesus Christ our Lord. Amen.

Just in case you are wondering how this was put together: the opening is from the psalms and is used at every Office of the Liturgy of the Hours. Repeat the Jesus Prayer eight times to symbolize Jesus Christ through whom, and in the Spirit, we hope to see the Father. (See "Patterns in the Church's Liturgy" for the significance of symbolizing the Incarnation, life, death, and Resurrection of Jesus with the "eighth day," or eighth age of creation, or simply the number eight). The final prayer is the Way of Beauty program, a prayer for artists. The wording was guided and approved by a trusted Dominican. We all seek inspiration and beauty in our activities, whatever we are doing, so this prayer can work for anyone on any day of the week. Of course, you may substitute any suitable invocation.

THE JESUS PRAYER AND MENTAL PRAYER

The second way to use this prayer is as meditation. It is said quietly (very quietly—perhaps one might say even that is "thought loudly"). In the Eastern Church, the faithful often pray a set number each day, guided by their spiritual director, using a black rope bracelet to count to the number of repetitions as they go. During quiet moments you could close your eyes and repeat this prayer. In the Eastern Church the words are timed with inhalation and exhalation to represent the unity of flesh and spirit: *Jesus Christ* (breath) ... *Son of God* (breath) ... *have mercy on me* (breath) ... *a sinner.*

Those experienced in praying this prayer agree that with many repetitions there is a steady calming, until the mind rests in silence on Jesus. It is a fully receptive state of prayer that allows the anxious mind to sense the presence of God.

This simple invocation of faith developed in the tradition of prayer under many forms in East and West. The most usual formulation, transmitted by the spiritual writers of the Sinai, Syria, and Mt. Athos, is the invocation, "Lord Jesus Christ, Son of God, have mercy on us sinners." It combines the Christological hymn of *Philippians* 2:6–11 with the cry of the publican and the blind men begging for light. By it the heart is opened to human wretchedness and the Savior's mercy.

The invocation of the holy name of Jesus is the simplest way of praying always. When the holy name is repeated often by a humbly attentive heart, the prayer is not lost by heaping up empty phrases, but holds fast to the word and "brings forth fruit with patience." This prayer is possible "at all times" because it is not one occupation among others but the only occupation: that of loving God, which animates and transfigures every action in Christ Jesus. (CCC 2667–2668)

APPENDIX C

❧

THE SACRED HEART

A DEEPENING DEVOTION

by David Clayton

As a convert to Catholicism, I was never attracted to the devotion to the Sacred Heart. Either the images looked too gruesome —a man with his beating, all-too-realistic heart held out in his hand—or too sentimental, not realistic enough.

Devotion to the Sacred Heart is quite ancient; it's implicit in the wound Jesus received in His side on the Cross. We find the idea going back at least to St. Gertrude in the thirteenth century, but of course, it's St. Margaret Mary Alacoque in the seventeenth century whose visions were the catalyst for its popularity today.

I have discovered that, far from being a shallow distraction, the devotion to the Sacred Heart goes to the core of what it means to relate to God. Fr. John Hardon says, "In my forty-two years in the priesthood I have dealt with many souls and have been involved in many problems. I believe the hardest mystery we are called on to believe, when everything is against it, is that God does love us."[6] The Sacred Heart rectifies the fundamental error of thinking we lack the free will to respond to God's heart, human and divine, of love for us.

My personal experience with this devotion began when I became lecturer at the Maryvale Institute in Birmingham. While there. I was asked to paint an image of the Sacred Heart to commemorate the twenty-fifth anniversary of the founding of the college.

Ever since its founding, like any educational institution seeking to be orthodox, it had had to counter efforts to undermine its

---

6 John Hardon, S.J., "Doctrinal Foundation of Devotion to the Sacred Heart," in *Faith & Reason* (Summer 1990).

mission. Fr. Paul Watson, the president of the college, explained to me that they felt sure that much of their success could be attributed to the protection of Christ through devotion to his Sacred Heart. The painting I did was presented to the college at the Silver Jubilee Mass.

Subsequently, I went to work at Thomas More College of Liberal Arts in New Hampshire. Like the Maryvale Institute, the college was asserting its Catholic identity and fidelity to the Magisterium and meeting with some resistance. Shortly after I arrived, I was struck one day by the words of the psalmist in the prayers of the Hour of None: "Vain is the builder's toil, if the house is not the Lord's building; vainly the guard keeps watch, if the city has not the Lord for its guardian" (cf. Ps. 127).

Recalling my experience at the Maryvale Institute, I immediately suggested to President William Fahey that we obtain an image of the Sacred Heart for our chapel at Thomas More. He had been thinking along similar lines. He told me that in fact his intention was, starting that fall, to dedicate the college each year to the care of the Sacred Heart of Jesus. The college has been rededicated each year since.

After every Mass we pray: "Sacred Heart of Jesus, in Your mercy, hear our prayer" as we turn to face the image of the Sacred Heart.

Sometime after this, Cardinal Raymond Burke, Prefect of the Supreme Tribunal of the Apostolic Signatura, spoke at a fundraising dinner for the college. The cardinal has a deep devotion to the Sacred Heart and was handing out prayer cards depicting the mosaic in his private chapel, which is a beautiful image.

Every time I have painted or drawn images associated with the devotion, it has reinforced my habit of praying to the Sacred Heart. I don't do any of the set devotions that many do—for example, the First Friday devotion. Maybe I will come to these in time. But I have a copy of my own icon on my home altar, and at the end of every Office that I pray, I pray to the Sacred Heart three times.

I can't describe any emotional experience associated with it or any miraculous event that has happened as result of prayer—that I'm aware of. However, it has become a habit that gives reassurance of God's love for me, especially when things seem difficult.

In the Liturgy of the Hours, when the psalms refer to God's great mercy, especially psalm 135, which starts and repeats often, "Praise the Lord, for he is good; for his mercy endureth forever," I see the picture of the Sacred Heart in my mind. When I look at a picture of the Sacred Heart, I think of His boundless mercy.

Sacred Heart of Jesus, in Your mercy, hear our prayer.

Sacred Heart of Jesus, in Your mercy, hear our prayer.

Sacred Heart of Jesus, in Your mercy, hear our prayer.

Appendix D

※

Patterns in the Church's Liturgy

by David Clayton

The worship of God in the Sacred Liturgy follows a pattern that is beautiful. When we participate, we open ourselves up to that pattern. Its beauty draws us to God and, in turn, transforms us.

Beauty appeals to what is ordered in us. Orderliness suggests pattern. There is pattern in everything created, including prayer. Where we find it, we respond to this pattern of prayer intuitively — whether we are aware of it or not. Conforming to its structure deepens our natural capacity to love and our intuitive sense of what is beautiful. We are made by God to desire wisdom and to be nourished by it *in that way*; and we respond to its particular beauty.

Furthermore, when this is presented in its appropriate context, in the Liturgy, which itself conforms to these patterns, the power is multiplied many times over.

Just by following along with the life of the Church, we will be living this pattern. All the aspects of Sacred Liturgy are in harmony, and whether we know of it or not, we are hearing this mystical music and are benefitting from it. Even those without faith have a glimmering of this pattern of life, and intuitively they respond to the order that underlies it. A life that conforms to this liturgical pattern bears the mark of the pattern of heaven, what Pope Emeritus Benedict XVI, in *The Spirit of the Liturgy*, called a glimpse into the mind of the Creator.

TO-ING AND FRO-ING: THE RHYTHM OF *EXIT* AND *RETURN*

One pattern in Christian life is a two-way rhythm. We know that the Eucharist is the source and summit of a fully human and integrated life. All truly Christian activity, even outside the Sacred Liturgy, is derived from it and nourished by it, and in turn prepares us for a fruitful participation in the Liturgy. For example, when we offer charity to others, we grow in love—and in our capacity to offer more back to the Father when we return to worship Him.

We worship God in the Sacred Liturgy, this transforms us, and we are joined supernaturally to the transfigured Christ. Then we are dismissed and exit the temple to go into the world to love and serve the Lord by loving each other; and in our doing this, Christ loves through us. Each act of love deepens and intensifies what happened before and prepares us further for the next part of the cycle.

This cycle is spatial and temporal. We leave the place of worship and return. The time period of the week revolves around Sunday Mass—we exit it in time and then return to Sunday a week later. Or perhaps we don't wait a week before we return to worship. Going to daily Mass brings Sunday into an hour of an ordinary day. Then we are bringing Sunday Mass out into the week and all the places we go: time is named and organized so that we can follow this pattern. The Liturgy of the weekdays, especially the Liturgy of the Hours, makes this possible, grace-wise. And then there are even prayers for in between the Liturgy of the Hours to keep the Eucharist front and center.

Similarly, for many of our activities, there is a to-ing and fro-ing between the introspective,

interior prayer life and the outward directed active life. We can pray by turning inward to the place where God resides, listening to His still, small voice; we can pray more actively by singing our praises out loud. Each one simultaneously builds on and is nourished by the last, and contributes to and nourishes the next.

The duties of almsgiving and charity can have these two aspects as well. We can have a public life of service to others and the Church, which, although humbly offered, is meant to be visible so that its example can attract others to Christ. But there is also a more private, hidden side of charity, which is carried out unknown to most and even sometimes to those who benefit.

Even eating an ordinary meal shares in the pattern of fasting and feasting. In one, we deny ourselves so that our hunger reminds us (among other things) of our need for God and our reliance on Him for everything, including our "daily bread." This is often a more private, introspective process. When we feast, we feast with others, enjoying the gifts that God has given us in a way that is imbued with the spiritual meaning of the Holy Day.

THE PATTERN OF THE COSMOS AND THE LITURGY OF THE HOURS

The liturgical life very strikingly follows other cyclical patterns of beauty that we can draw from Tradition and find affirmed by Scripture. We notice rhythms and patterns of creation — the *cosmos* — especially in the motion of the sun and the moon in the sky. The Greek word *cosmos* means both "beauty" and "order." We use this same word in English to signify the order that runs through the universe, perceptible to us. Our wonder at this order is part of what we experience when we call something beautiful.

Traditionally, the heavens were seen as a sign of the pattern of heaven beyond. The heavenly liturgy, the dynamic of love between God and all His saints and angels, is the standard that informs everything. The earthly Liturgy is a supernatural step into the heavenly Liturgy, and another reinforcing cycle is complete. The cosmos is a sign that helps us to order our lives here on earth so that they are in harmony with the pattern of heaven. The sun, especially the rising sun in the east, signifies the Light of the World, the Son. This is why churches are oriented toward the east: so that we all look expectantly for the coming of the Son.

There is a pattern to the calendar. The months come from an idealized pattern of the moon's waxing and waning, and the year relates to the cycle of the earth's motion around the sun. There is the pattern to the seasons of the Church with Easter at the center. Certain hours of the day follow the pattern of the Hours of the Divine Office, and the weekly cycle follows a pattern with Sunday Mass at its center.

A priest friend gave us a beautiful image of this truth: "The Mass is a jewel in its setting and that setting is the Liturgy of the Hours; and the whole Sacred Liturgy is in turn a jewel in its setting, which is the cosmos." It is interesting that chronologically the setting for each was made before its corresponding jewel. The Creator made the cosmos before man prayed to Him. Jews prayed the original Liturgy of the Hours, which in its essence is the Old Testament praying of the psalms and the marking of the Hours, before the coming of Christ. Last, in time, was the institution of the ultimate jewel, the Mass.

OUR PATTERN OF PRAYER WILL GOVERN THE PATTERN OF OUR LIVES

If we begin by conforming our prayer life to the heavenly patterns, with our worship in the Liturgy given the highest priority, we will find that quite naturally the rest of our daily activities will be permeated with this liturgical order. Man is made to worship God. He even works better when his work is nourished by a balance of prayer and rest, in conformity with this natural pattern of worship — although, that is a happy side effect. (It would be a perversion to worship and rest in order to work better! Worship and rest are higher than work.)

Nevertheless, it's interesting to see that work begins to recover some of its prelapsarian characteristics when man worships and rests well.

SEVENS AND EIGHTS

Let's look at another pattern, that of sevens and eights. The book of Genesis describes the institution of seven in the Creation story; the symbolism is reinforced with the appearance of the seven-color rainbow in the sky when Noah is saved and the covenant with all the earth is reinstituted.

Eight is the number of new covenant ushered in with the Incarnation, life, death, and Resurrection of Christ. These events take the seven days and add to them the eighth: the Sunday of Christ's rising — the new day —which is simultaneously the first day of the next week and the last, that is to say, the eighth, of the previous one. The transition of the old to the new is symbolized by the operation of adding one to seven. Thus, eight is the number we associate with the Liturgy, since it is the number of the new covenant.

A covenant is a reciprocal relationship, sealed by an oath. We are used to the idea of agreements linked to exchange. Most of these are contractual: each party agrees to do something on the condition that he receives something in return. However, contracts are crucially different from covenants. Whereas a contract is an alignment of self-interest, so that each party gets out of it what he wants for himself, a covenant is one of alignment of interest in the other. It is mutual self-gift in which each *gives* to the other. In its highest form, the person gives the gift of himself; this is the form of the love between the persons of the Trinity. To give an illustration in our own experience: a Christian marriage is covenantal. A prenuptial agreement is contractual.

In our relationship with God, He has already given Himself to us. We have freedom, so we are not bound to respond, but if we do, the appropriate response is contained within the sevenfold pattern of action in the Liturgy set down for us from the book of Genesis onward. Scott Hahn describes this in his book *Letter and Spirit*: "The Hebrew for seven, sheva, has a verb form. Sheva is the verb for swearing oath. Its meaning is to 'seven' oneself. When human beings swear in this way, they follow the precedent set by God at the dawn of Creation."[7]

Seven is the number of God's covenantal oath. Interestingly, in the book of Revelation we find the consummation of the covenant expressed many ways in the symbolism of seven (e.g., churches, spirits, torches, lamp stands). Of course, all of these sevens are fulfilled in the eight (symbolizing the new covenant that unites the old, the seven, with the One, Christ): Christ Himself, who sits in glory in heaven.

---

[7] Hahn, *Letter and Spirit*, 60.

TIME GOES FORWARD IN A HELIX: DAYS, WEEKS, SEASONS, YEARS

This idea of cycles governed by seven and eight creates a picture of a progression that is helical, rather than linear. As each day moves forward in time, we can imagine a vector shift that is forward and upward and turns an angle, so that by the time eight days have progressed, a full circle has been turned and the eighth is directly above the first. We have traced out seven days of the week, and then the significant addition of another day takes us to another Sunday, sitting vertically above the previous Sunday, which is a pitch of the thread beneath it. So, although this new day retains the character of any earlier Sunday (derived from *the* Sunday, Easter, Christ's Resurrection day), it is also a *new* Sunday. It simultaneously marks the end of the last week and the beginning of the next, putting it at the center of the liturgical rhythm of the week. You might say that Sunday is the Day of days.

This way, the liturgical weekly cycle traces a holy spiral upward to heaven. All we have to do is participate in the liturgical life, and we are transported along this path to heaven.

In the context of the year, Easter is at the center. At any point before, we are in anticipation of it, and any point after, in celebration of it. If Sunday is the Day of days, Easter Sunday is the Sunday of Sundays!

To emphasize this, there are eight consecutive eighth days in the octave of Easter (and we see this with the other high feast, Christmas). Such an octave is in effect a week of Sundays. Prior to Easter there are (an idealized) seven weeks of Lent (it is actually a couple of days short of a complete seven) and afterward there are the fifty days of Easter, culminating in Pentecost. The period from Easter to Pentecost consists of seven weeks of seven days, forty-nine days in all, which are brought to completion by the addition of an eighth day at the end. Here we have a pattern: seven is the number that signifies the old covenant, and eight is the number that represents its fulfillment in Christ.

This pattern of seven being resolved in eight is present within the structure of each day as well. Quoting Psalm 118 in chapter 16 of his Rule, St. Benedict establishes the eight traditional Offices (seven daytime and one nighttime) and their hours in the Divine Office:

Now the sacred number of seven will be fulfilled by us if we perform the Offices of our service at the time of the Morning Office, Prime, Terce, Sext, None, Vespers, and Compline, since it was of these day Hours that he said, "Seven times in the day I have rendered praise to You" [Ps. 118:164]. For as to the Night Office the same Prophet says, "In the middle of the night I arose to glorify You"

[Ps. 118:62]. Let us therefore bring our tribute of praise to our Creator "for the judgments of His justice" at these times: the Morning Office, Prime, Terce, Sext, None, Vespers, and Compline; and in the night let us arise to glorify Him.

Taking all of these thoughts into account, we can see that the prayer of the Church, which is the prayer of Christ Himself ushering the world forward on a path of redemption through sacred time, is a triple helix. The tight daily helix spirals its way on the weekly helix, which in turn sits on the giant helix that rotates once a year.

In a sermon for Low Sunday (the Sunday after Easter), from the Office of Readings for that day, eight days after Easter, St. Augustine tells us how the octave was anticipated in the Old Testament:

> This is the octave day of your new birth. Today is fulfilled in you the sign of faith that was prefigured in the Old Testament by the circumcision of the flesh on the eighth day after birth. When the Lord rose from the dead, he put off the mortality of the flesh; his risen body was still the same body, but it was no longer subject to death. By his resurrection he consecrated Sunday, or the Lord's Day. Though the third after his passion, this day is the eighth after the Sabbath, and thus also the first day of the week.

PERFECT, SUPERFLUOUS, AND DIMINISHED NUMBERS

There is another sort of number in the Liturgy and our ordering of time: a "perfect" number. Because we can numerically describe the beauty of the order of the cosmos, the Fathers found patterns of beauty and symmetry even there and saw correspondences between the cosmos and the Liturgy. A perfect number is one that is "the sum of its aliquot parts."

Unless you are already familiar with ancient mathematical treatises, that phrase probably means nothing! But in fact it is quite simple, and we can understand it if we look at the example of the first perfect number, 6. The aliquots parts of 6 are those numbers that can be multiplied by a whole number to give a product of 6: 1, 2, and 3. Six is perfect because it is the sum of 1, 2, and 3. In fact, even among perfect numbers, it has a higher degree of perfection in that it is also the product of 1, 2, and 3. It is both the product and the sum of its aliquot parts. The number 6 has biblical significance because the work of creation was carried out in six days.

St. Augustine notes this connection and sees the arithmetic principle as the governing principle. In the *City of God* he says: "Six is a number that is perfect in itself, and not because God created the world in six days: rather the contrary is true. God created the world in six days because this number is perfect, and it would remain perfect, even if the work of the six days did not exist" (bk. 11, chap. 30).

The application of this understanding is the ordering of human time into seven-day weeks—six days of work and one day of rest, following the pattern with which God created the world. There is a spiritual significance ascribed to this. Those numbers whose sum is greater or less than their aliquot parts are called superfluous or diminished, respectively. Boethius, a sixth-century philosopher, explains, drawing on the Aristotelian spirit of the temperate mean, that perfect numbers are considered so as a consequence of their relationship with superfluous and diminished numbers: "Between these two kinds of number, as if between two elements unequal and intemperate, is put a number which holds the middle place between the extremes, like one who seeks virtue."[8]

The second perfect number is twenty-eight (1+2+4+7+14=28). An idealized lunar month is twenty-eight days. The month contains within it this same pattern of the to-ing and fro-ing because it has two phases (a waxing and a waning—new moon to new moon or full moon to full moon); and the seven-day week is half a phase. The moon is traditionally seen as the symbol of the Church, and it governs the seasons of the liturgy, most especially Easter.

When the Divine Office according the Roman Rite was revised after the Second Vatican Council, it was ordered around a twenty-eight-day cycle, according with traditional principles. The connection with the lunar cycle is scriptural, incidentally: "He made the moon also, to serve in its season to mark the times and to be an everlasting sign. From the moon comes the sign for feast days, a light that wanes when it has reached the full. The month is named for the moon, increasing marvelously in its phases, an instrument of the hosts on high shining forth in the firmament of heaven" (Sir. 43:6–8).

THE SPECIAL VALUE OF THE PSALMS

The psalms inform liturgical prayer. A significant proportion of the Liturgy quotes them directly, including many of the prayers. Although the book of Psalms is in the Old Testament, it anticipates and foreshadows the New. In his commentary on the Psalms, St. Thomas Aquinas tells us that this book encompasses the wisdom of theology: "The material is universal, for while the particular books of the Canon of Scripture contain special materials, this book has the general material of Theology as a whole." Then in referring to their special place in the Liturgy where they are to be sung, he says, "This is what Dionysius [the Areopagite] says in Book 3 of the Celestial Hierarchy:

---

8 In Michael Masi, *Boethian Number Theory: A Translation of De Institutione Arithmetica* (Amsterdam: Rodopi Press, 1983), 96.

the sacred scripture of the Divine Songs (the Psalms) is intended to sing of all sacred and divine workings" (Introduction to St. Thomas's *Exposition of the Psalms of David*).

Like the Liturgy as a whole, the psalms participate in this twofold dynamic (the "to-ing and fro-ing" again) of prayer. The *Catechism* tells us that the psalms "both nourish and express our prayer." That is, they simultaneously articulate what we want to say *and* answer our prayer. And like the Liturgy, the psalms are "inseparably personal and communal ... prayed by Christ and fulfilled in Him ... essential to the prayer of the Church" (CCC 2586).

Those who pray the psalms regularly will tell you of the extraordinary way in which a psalm seems to speak to them, articulating their concerns, worries, thoughts, and feelings. We can identify with the person expressing them. Then, with the psalmist, we call out to God; and then the prayer is answered. Genuine consolation and peace arise from this prayer. More than honeyed words, there is substance beneath them; and they open us up to it.

Given that the psalms contain "the whole of theology," there is a profound wisdom that can be brought to bear on all aspects of human life through them. It impresses itself upon our hearts in the Sacred Liturgy. St. Thomas goes on to explain that the very structure of the book of Psalms conforms to the symbolism of the numbers seven and eight:

The first distinction is that there are one hundred and fifty psalms; this is a mystery, because this number is composed of 70 and 80. By 7, from which 70 is named, the course of this time is signified, which is carried out in seven days; by 8, from which 80 is named, the state of the future life. For the number eight according to the Gloss[9] concerns those who rise from the dead; and it signifies that in this book there is a treatment of those things that pertain to the course of the present life, and to future glory. Again, by seven the Old Testament is signified. The fathers of the Old Testament observed that which is seventh: they observed the seventh day, the seventh week, the seventh month, and the seventh year of the seventh decade, which is called the Jubilee. By eight the New Testament is signified: we celebrate the eighth day, namely the Lord's Day, on account of the solemnity of the Lord's resurrection; and in this book are contained the mysteries of the Old and New Testament.

This 7:8 structure, then, is a ratio that signifies faithful anticipation and then fulfillment;

---

[9] The Gloss is the *glossa ordinaria*, a standard biblical commentary based on teachings of the Fathers, predominantly Jerome, Augustine, Bede, and Gregory.

we see it represented in the Lent/Easter/Pentecost relationship already described; and in the Old/New Testament covenantal relationship that St. Thomas describes. There is another mystery at work here. Sevenfold repetition is traditionally seen as one way of effecting a continuous activity or perfecting an action: "The promises of the LORD are promises that are pure, silver refined in a furnace on the ground, purified seven times" (Ps. 12:6). Purified seven times means perfectly refined; that is, pure. And as St. Augustine says, "I will praise you seven times a day" means exactly the same as "his praise is always on my lips,"[10] and then on the eighth (Sunday, the day of worship in the Eucharist), the praise is consecrated to God.

PATTERNS IN MUSIC

There is another amazing manifestation of this pattern of seven and eight in the beauty of music. If we talk of octaves, most people assume we are talking about music; and of course we find that the beautiful patterns of harmony in music do occur in octaves. The traditional Western musical scale has seven notes, and the eighth is higher still, simultaneously the last note of the previous octave and the first of the next.

Going further, within music, harmonious relationships can be described numerically by considering the relative lengths of pieces of string (or lengths of pitch pipe) that produce particular notes when plucked (or blown). To describe the interval of an octave, you would have one string twice the length of another, so this means that the ratio 1:2 is another way of demonstrating an octave. It is interesting that physics reveals this proportion, yielding the concept of an octave, although it's not clear why simply dividing the string in half makes it sound "the same, only lower." Yet everyone in every culture and every age has heard it thus.

We can think of a high and a low C as a musical equivalent—an analogy—of Easter Sunday and Low Sunday. Just as the human intellect is made to hear a special relationship between the two notes, so the natural rhythm of worship is this pattern of seven and eight.

As many will know, the other fundamental music harmonies with the octave, the fourth and the fifth, produce ratios of 3:4 and 2:3.

The ancient musical scales in which the psalms are sung are called modes. And it should be no surprise that there are eight modes in traditional plainchant. Conventional music uses only two modes—which we refer to as major and minor keys. Traditional music has six more. Although chant sounds simple, the patterns of notes and harmonic relationships express musically and very deeply the cosmic beauty which, of course, points to the heavenly beauty. This is why chant is a formation in beauty.

---

[10] St. Augustine, *On Christian Teaching*, trans. R.P.H. Green (Oxford: Oxford University Press, 1997), 62.

A common pattern of beauty runs through the structure of the Liturgy (daily, weekly, seasonal, and annual), that is, the text of the psalms and the music to which they are sung—and, ideally, even the church building in which we sing them. What might seem at first the ordinary act of chanting a psalm to its simple tone while marking the Hour is in fact invoking a whole host of intertwining harmonious relationships. We hear only one note at a time; yet the whole speaks to us of something that is dazzling in its beauty and complexity. The wonder of all of this is that God made us so that we can grasp this effortlessly. Our minds apprehend the silent symphony. This makes our praise of God deep and powerful, the song of life that is played out in our day.

THE PATTERN IN CULTURE

There are many of these patterns that run through the Liturgy (probably many that I don't know about). But while it can be helpful to be consciously aware of them (especially if we are artists, architects, or musicians), it is not absolutely necessary. We don't need to be thinking sevens and eights (or twos) to benefit from this patterned reality.

Just by doing our best to conform to the pattern of the Liturgy, as set out by the Church, we are opening our souls to the beauty of heaven and forming our intuitive sense of what is beautiful as well. This in turn guides our natural preferences when we go out into the world so that they become more beautiful and more graceful. Consequently, our part in making the culture will reflect the beauty of God and this will, we hope, draw others to Him.

Where these patterns are known and used consciously the effect can be wonderful too. For example, for centuries architects have used numerical relationships just like this to dictate the size of buildings. This is why most old buildings (not just churches) look beautiful to us: they are conforming to this liturgical and cosmic beauty, so the whole environment speaks subtly of our heavenly destiny. We can't help but pick it up because we are hardwired to see it, whether we are aware of it or not.

It is also the reason so many modern buildings lack beauty. Architects no longer learn the traditional proportions and instead think that they can invent their own order. What they don't realize is that there is no order outside the divine order; there is only disorder and ugliness.

We can order all time and space according to numerical relationships. The symbolism of eight and seven is only one example that could govern beauty—there are many more. Finding them is what makes human creativity so exciting and rewarding—delving into these patterns, understanding them better, ultimately making them part of the culture. Potentially, all human activity can conform to cosmic patterns established by God, forming the basis of a traditional culture of beauty.

APPLYING BEAUTIFUL PATTERNS IN BUSINESS

A CASE STUDY

by David Clayton

When James Woodward decided to open a second high-end men's clothes shop he wanted to model it upon the principles he had read about on my site, "The Way of Beauty." In his first shop, in Oxted in the county of Surrey in England (about an hour from London), these principles had yielded encouraging results, although existing conditions had allowed him to implement them only partially. Nevertheless, he thought that the changes he was able to make were effective.

The local bank manager had told him at one point, in the deepest part of the recession, that James's was the only business on his books that showed any significant signs of growth. "I had been making money, and I felt that your principles had contributed. The growth of the business is helping to fund the investment in this new shop. But it isn't just the money," he told me. "The principles that I had been able to try seemed to show me a way of having the values of my Catholic Faith penetrate the everyday activities of business much more deeply than before."

Now, because he was beginning afresh in this new venture, he saw the opening of his second shop in Banstead, also in the county of Surrey, as an opportunity to use the ideas more fully. So he telephoned me to ask for ideas about the layout and decoration.

James converted to the Catholic Faith about fifteen years ago. I had known him first through the London Oratory. We had stayed in touch after I left London and moved to the United

States and had had several conversations about the Way of Beauty over the years. He was aware that beauty could have an impact on every aspect of life.

Here's what I suggested to him: Always ask the question, "Is this beautiful?" And be prepared to go against the trend of modern design if necessary.

I offered some specific points:

• The general design ought to give a general impression of symmetry and order, but within this, introduce *some* details of asymmetry. Too much rigid symmetry is cold and sterile. James went directly against the advice of his retail designers here, who recommended more sweeping and turning curves in the layout.

• I suggested that the color scheme should be based on muted natural earth colors, if possible, to ensure color harmony. This scheme showcases the brightly colored clothing he sells; thus, his merchandise, rather than the paint on the walls, attracts the eye.

• I urge the use of natural materials where possible. Real wood and natural fibers give a sense of belonging and fittingness to an environment. Lighting is important as well, with incandescent lights being far more flattering and peaceful than compact fluorescent ones.

• As the clothes are presented on shelves, I suggested that the spacing of the shelves should not be even, but should vary so that the largest spacing is at the bottom and smallest at the top, mimicking the proportions of storey size in traditional architecture. These proportions are ancient and traditional design principles, found as far back as Vitruvius's first-century architecture treatise and Boethius's sixth-century works. They are used in Gothic cathedrals and in ancient town houses. The usual experts in interior design fought him, but Jim stuck to his guns.

• I encouraged the use of the natural beauty of plants in the shop too—potted plants and cut flowers. Because there are people walking around the shop, this meant that he had to incorporate in the layout spaces and shelves just for this purpose, so that the arrangements could be placed without impeding the flow of people or the views of the clothes he was selling.

• I told him to try to avoid pop or rock music, instead opting for something beautiful and serene. I am not completely against all popular music per se, nor do I think it all ugly, but even good music that is fun for dancing at midnight is unlikely to promote calm and peace, which is what we were aiming for the shop. In the end, James decided on no music at all. Once more, he was taking a risk. Almost all retailers install music systems and recommend constant background music. The thinking is that such music causes people to buy more quickly. Some of the staff who enjoyed listening to pop music while they worked initially resisted his decision, but Jim persuaded them of the value of what he was doing.

• I believe that it is important to have the face of Christ as a focal point in the décor (a good principle for all main rooms in a building). James bought a small icon of the Mandylion (the image of the face of Christ on the veil of Veronica) and put it on the wall behind the cash register. Thus, every customer going to the counter would very likely notice it in some way, yet its size and traditional quality would not be perceived as aggressive. In his previous shop, James also put a nativity scene in the window every Christmas, a custom he will continue. Aside from any thoughts about décor, he wanted to bear witness to his faith in an open but understated way. Again, the advice of the professionals is the exact opposite! Their view is that it would offend and repel non-Christians. However, he has had no complaints from customers—and several complimentary remarks. Small children even pulled their parents into the shop as a result of the nativity in the window.

• Finally, I suggested that he pray the Liturgy of the Hours as part of his spiritual life, even trying to mark each Hour with a prayer of some sort if time was short. He might, I thought, consciously dedicate this prayer as a sacrifice for the well-being of his employees and his customers.

Jim implemented everything in line with my guidelines. The shelves are oak veneer, and the flooring is solid oak coupled with pure wool carpeting. The paintwork is all naturally hued traditional paint. What is interesting to me is that the shop does not look like a re-creation of a quaint faux-Dickens "Ye Olde English" shop. Rather, he has incorporated these ideas into a clean-cut modern style. This enhancement of the modern with traditional ideas is very powerful. Clearly, using these high-quality materials involves a greater outlay than the usual materials: I wondered if he felt that the extra investment had been worthwhile.

"The look of the place has had an impact. Several customers and other local retailers have complimented the shop, actually using the word *beautiful*. For example, I was at the local newsagents, and the lady behind the till engaged me in conversation. When she realized I was from the new Woodward Menswear, she immediately told me that people had been saying to her how beautiful the shop was. Many customers have told me how comfortable and inviting the shop is, and one top-notch fellow fashion retailer said it was a really beautiful shop and 'very calming.' I think that praying for the customers and the staff has helped in many ways. Of course, it might be that my managerial skills have just improved with experience, but recruiting and keeping staff was something that I had found very difficult. Without knowing why, this is something that seems to have become easier. I can't speak for them of course, but my sense is that both shops have become happier places to work."

And the bottom line?

"I am very pleased. After a couple of years, I am making as much money as my first shop, which I bought as a business of thirty years' standing and had been running for several years. This is better than I had expected. Of course, these beautiful features are not the only thing that will be contributing to the business. I have learnt a lot about retail while running my first shop and so have put many lessons into practice in this second. I still had to get the location and the stock right, along with all the other business variables. However, if it's only for the comments and my own pleasure at working in such a lovely environment, I definitely feel that it has been worthwhile."

This seems to have contributed to a new venture. Earlier this year, out of the blue, a very successful supplier who had been impressed with Jim's shops and the way he did business approached him. He wanted to know if Jim wanted to join forces with him to start supplying high-quality German trousers to American retailers. After these initial discussions, a new company has been created; they are now the sole distributers for a German clothes manufacturer.

"I am excited about this new development," Jim told me. "I want to make sure that I make the principles of the Way of Beauty work in this new business as well. I have a feeling that I am just scratching the surface so far."

Bringing the Little Oratory to the Community

Taking Vespers to the Veterans Hospital

by David Clayton

Recently when I went home to England, we had a reunion of old college friends. Most were not believers of any sort. I had known them since I was eighteen, and so the friendships predated, by a long way, my conversion (I was thirty-one when I was received into the Church). It was great to catch up with everyone and see how they were getting on.

I was interested by a recent decision of one. She had given up teaching genetics to graduate students at Imperial College, London, and was now working for a company that would teach executives at investment banks in London how to meditate. The banks were prepared to pay for this because they thought it would help

them deal with the stress of the job. She had learned to meditate when she took up yoga. Her initial interest had been in the physical benefits; soon she delved into the spirituality that is attached to it.

To convince the executives that there is something to this Eastern meditation, the meditation teachers come armed with statistics from scientific research, according to which there are observable improvements in the condition of heart patients in hospitals when people meditate. Even when the patients do not meditate with the teachers, even if they were unaware that it is happening, just to have meditation going on in the building has a positive effect.

I saw no reason to doubt what she said about the effect of Eastern meditation in hospitals. I believed her when she said that the research backed her up. However, my reaction was that if anything good was coming out of this, then it was because it was participating in some way in Christian prayer, whether they knew it or not. Whatever benefits there were would be greater through the full expression of what that meditation was attempting to achieve. If someone did traditional Western Christian prayer, I would expect even greater things.

When I got back to the United States, I contacted local hospitals and asked if they would like a small group of people to come and sing Vespers on a regular basis. What is surprising (and some ways dismaying) is that I couldn't find anyone who had ever heard of this being done before. There are Christian prayer groups who visit hospitals, but I haven't heard of people making a regular commitment (beyond the occasional concert) to pray the Liturgy of the Hours for these communities. Shouldn't the Divine Office be one of our most powerful weapons in evangelization?

I didn't expect anyone to welcome us with open arms. All I wanted was for us to be tolerated, so that we could pray the Office for and with those in the hospital. I didn't mind if nobody else attended—we wanted to pray for them regardless.

The point in my mind was to make the personal sacrifice in prayer, praying for the well-being of the patients and for the hospital as a community.

There is an important point to make here. While the fruits of Sacred Liturgy, such as charity toward our brethren, are great, they are not the ultimate goal. We wanted to make sure that in bringing this prayer and work of charity to the hospital, the driving principle was the worship of God. Accordingly, we make every effort to chant beautifully for God, regardless of how many others attend.

I was delighted when the Catholic chaplain at the Veterans Administration Hospital in Manchester, New Hampshire, invited us to come in every other Monday evening. Fr. Boucher is an old friend of mine and of the college where I teach, Thomas More College of Liberal Arts. For a year now, at the time of writing, Fr. Boucher, Dr. Tom Larson, also from the college, any students who are available to come—usually three or four—and I have been singing Vespers and Compline twice a month on Monday evenings. Because the Liturgy of the Hours is quintessentially ecumenical, we were able to fill an available administrative slot in the chaplaincy, and a few non-Catholics have joined us.

Although most patients know we are doing this, they are for the most part too ill or injured even to be able to get up one floor from the ward without someone dressing them and bringing them up, and those helpers aren't always available. Still, we aren't under the impression that large numbers want to come but can't make it. Sometimes a few come, sometimes none. Those who are able to come are in wheelchairs, and we might see one person two or three times at most. Often Fr. Boucher will lead us in prayer for those who have died in the past few days in the hospital.

On more than one occasion, only the three of us (plus Tom's son, Ben) will be present, but we pray anyway. For the Magnificat, the Nunc Dimittis, the Our Father, and the St. Michael Prayer we sing four-part harmonies arranged by Paul Jernberg (information about this composer is in the resources and highly recommended). We keep the door open, singing loudly enough so that the sound floats down the corridor for the wards to hear. Those who come are always surprised at the effort we make to sing well on their behalf and to praise God. It has been gratifying to hear how readily those who come sing, and want to—even though many have never prayed any Office before. We are singing in English, so any visitor can understand and join in. The singing has the feel of the plainchant modal tradition, which engages those who hear it.

I wouldn't go out and sing in public in this way if I didn't feel that what we have is beautiful, accessible, and fits naturally with the language. I have been part of processions in public before, cringing with embarrassment at the songs and having to offer the experience up as a penance in order to keep doing it. Unlike those occasions, I am happy to sing the chant because it feels vigorous and masculine, yet pious and respectful of God. (Remember, we are singing for soldiers!)

How does this compare in effect with Eastern meditation? I don't have any scientific research to make direct comparisons, but I can relate two anecdotes that give some evidence of a profound effect.

At some point during the year, a charismatic prayer group and a nurse, independently, found out about what we were doing and made an effort to wheel veterans to the chapel. So we were seeing three or four veterans and three or four from the prayer group and the nurse. Then the leader of the prayer group, Gene, told me of several patients who were so ill that they could not get out of bed. Would we go down to their rooms and sing for them after Vespers and Compline? Of course we agreed, and our little group went and sang the four-part versions of the Our Father and the St. Michael prayer. One week we went into six rooms.

Shortly afterward Gene asked me to lunch, because he had something to propose. When I met him, he told me that he was excited because he had been praying with patients in hospitals for a long time, and he could see that this Divine Office prayer was affecting the patients (and the nurses and staff) in a deep way. To him, it almost seemed miraculous; their spirits were raised so dramatically. He said that he had contacted his network throughout the state and he wanted to make sure that his prayer group was there too, visiting the wards, every time we sang in the hospital. He wanted to start a ministry in nursing homes, homes for the elderly, and hospitals. He said that the music was very beautiful and he had not heard anything like it before.

I suggested that we could see how it went, but as a start would he like me to teach his charismatic group to sing this chant? He didn't think it was possible. He doubted me when I told him that our chant is easier to sing than anything they currently sing at Mass. Nevertheless, we have had several singing classes at which everyone has done very well. After each class we sing Compline together.

Among the Thomas More College students who used to come with us when he could was a young man, George Paul, who has left the college to join the seminary. At the end of the academic year, he approached me with the news of his vocation. He told me that one of the best things he did at the college the previous year was singing Vespers at the VA hospital in Manchester. He had two friends already at the seminary, and they wanted to try to get something similar going. Could I help him?

Of course I could. I gave him the materials that we had been using and explained more deeply the philosophy behind what we do; and I told him how he could lead the prayer if they couldn't find a chaplain (remember, praying the Liturgy of the Hours does not require the presence of clergy).

If any readers wish to start something like this, I encourage you to do so. I will be pleased to hear from you if you need help. Contact me through my website: http://thewayofbeauty.org.

Appendix G

—————— ❧ ——————

Even You Can Sing!

A Guide for Singing for the Timid, the Tone-Deaf, and the Unlearned

by David Clayton

Any vocal prayer can be sung. Ideally, the Liturgy would be sung. This section is for those who wish they could sing, but don't know what to do or how to do it. I hope that through this learning process you will at least be able to make a start.

I didn't think I could chant my prayers, but I found a simple method that sounded good to me and meant that I could very quickly learn to sing the whole psalter. You can use the instructions here in conjunction with a page on my blog (http://thewayofbeauty.org) called Psalm Tones, which has recordings of the chants referred to, so that you can practice singing along.

PEOPLE (YES, EVEN MEN) LIKE TO SING

I used to be told that trying to get people to sing is a lost cause. Men won't sing, and especially British men won't sing (I am British, so I can say this). In fact, male singing is very much a part of British culture. Every week about seven hundred thousand people, mostly men, gather together in groups of up to sixty thousand and chant. I'm talking about the crowds at soccer matches. If you haven't attended a British soccer match, then you won't know that the level of singing is phenomenal. The content of the chant is unrepeatable, of course—usually it consists of abuse against the opposition and the match officials, and definitely could not be described as Gregorian—but it is led by men, and other men join in with hearty voices.

This is all very well, but does this participation in chant's rowdy counterpart indicate that people will be convinced to sing in church? I think that the answer is yes.

A few years ago, I met the pastor of Chicago's St. John Cantius parish, which has been spectacularly successful in attracting parishioners and raising vocations to the priesthood. From a congregation of about thirty souls a quarter of a century ago, it has grown to one of 3,500 families. Fr. C. Frank Philips attributes this growth in part to orthodoxy and beautiful Liturgy. At this church the Office is sung publicly, and parishioners join in.

I asked Fr. Philips for advice on getting people to sing at Thomas More College, where I teach, and he told me that if you want everyone to sing, then you must have a man leading. Regardless of how fair or unfair you think it is, he said, men just won't join in if a woman is leading; by having a female cantor, you are excluding half the congregation. Also, he said, the pitch must be at a natural level for a man who is not a strained high tenor but a baritone, to sing. In other words, get a man to lead and then sing at his natural pitch.

Interestingly, the physics of sound support this notion and make it seem less unfair. When a man sings a note in his natural (that is, low) range, the overtones of that note contain the notes from the higher registers as well, an octave or two above. Even in singing in unison, the lower note essentially contains the note sung an octave above (as well as the harmonic series of thirds and fifths) within it. So the male voice supports the woman's voice above it, whereas the woman's voice doesn't do the same for the man's.

If you have men leading, you don't worry about the women, because they are much more inclined to sing, more used to singing and hearing their own voices, and will always sing anyway. At least, if a woman leads, she should take care to choose a key that is accessible to men as well as women (and for that matter, for alto women!).

The challenge is to coax the men into singing; then all will sing. I followed his advice, and he was right.

FATHERS, IT'S YOUR RESPONSIBILITY ONCE AGAIN; BUT RELAX, WE'LL HELP YOU THROUGH IT

This means that, men, we would love to see you start stepping up and taking responsibility by singing at the domestic altar.

In the end, if this really is torture for you, no one can expect you to do it. But my experience is that most people really do like to sing and *would* sing if they thought they could. Some will need more help than a couple of pages here can provide, but I think that, after reading the following, most can do it.

WHAT SHOULD WE SING? CHANT!

There is one other condition that will help people get used to singing in church, and that is using chant. This will surprise many people who think chant is obscure and difficult, but it is in fact the easiest music to get people to join in.

In 1903 Pope Pius X wrote an instruction of sacred music called *Tra le Sollecitudini* that explains why Gregorian chant, which is proper to the Roman Church, is the highest form of sacred music. Gregorian chant was developed for the Latin language and, along with polyphony, is always recommended for the Latin liturgy without reservation. While we cannot use pure Gregorian chant in English, because the patterns of the two languages are different, we can use something close, derived from traditional forms.

Developing chant for English is a tradition in the making, and it can be hit or miss. The forms of chant we suggest for the English here have been tested, and I have witnessed them working. They are simple enough for nearly everyone to sing and beautiful enough for most people to want to sing.

Chant is certainly otherworldly—it speaks of another realm—but it is not difficult to do.

It is very natural to us. Of course, there are some very complex variations, but the simple forms are much easier to sing than any nearly all contemporary music that you hear in English-speaking churches. And if you use these simple forms, you will find that everybody is able to join in. Often, if they don't want to, it's because they assume that they aren't capable. My experience is that once they realize that they can, then their attitude changes. If you doubt this, read the account of our group that sings Vespers in the veterans hospital in Manchester, New Hampshire (see "Taking Vespers to the Veterans Hospital" in the appendix). Then, if you still don't believe me, give the tones we give you here a try, and see what you think!

IF YOU CAN TALK, YOU CAN CHANT

You may not realize that a big part of singing is listening. If you find it difficult to carry a tune, the first goal is to sing with others; but don't sing too quietly, and don't try to hide in the group. If you are worried that you are out of tune, fear of embarrassment will make you sing at a low volume. Ironically, this is likely to make things worse. You have to be able to sing loudly enough to hear yourself—otherwise you simply can't judge where you are in relation to others, thus making you more out of tune.

With improved listening as your goal, don't sing too loudly either. If you sing so loudly that you can't hear anyone else in the group, you have nothing to compare your own pitch with to see whether you are in tune. When we are learning, the way that we know we are in tune is by active listening—comparing what we are singing with someone else who is in tune. If you can hear both yourself and the other, then one of two things will happen. Either the others will move toward you, tune-wise, or else you will move toward the others. Usually, it is the latter!

If you can talk at all, then you can chant. Talking has a modulation in tone and is more complicated than singing on one note, and singing on one note is a traditional form of the simplest chant. It is so established as part of the tradition that there is even a Latin name for it: *recto tono*, meaning "straight tone."

As an exercise, try reading anything out loud at just the rhythm you would say it in natural speech, but all on one note. If you can do this, you are chanting.

Strange as it may seem, another thing to do is to practice singing on your own while singing on one note. Get used to hearing yourself sing without anybody else listening. I practiced this by memorizing some very simple chant I found on the Internet. And then I sang it loudly without anybody listening to me. Singing in the shower is perfect. I got used to hearing the sound of my own voice and listening to what I was singing.

It may seem strange, but before I started to do this, I had never really listened to myself

as I sang. It was an unnerving experience at first, because I couldn't stop imagining that someone might be listening. Then I would get nervous, my voice would drop in volume, and I would go off tune—even when that tune was one note!

When I noticed this happening, I had to tell myself that no one was listening, so it didn't matter, and then resume with greater gusto. Provided I was singing loudly enough, I found that I could hear if I was out of tune or wavering and actually correct myself. Also, I got used to singing in the pitch that was natural to me, so that I didn't have to strain my voice.

In fact, once you can sing *recto tono*, you can join in pretty much any other chant of the psalms as well (although chant in the Mass is probably a bit more complicated). There are many different melodies available for the psalms (the book we recommend has about 120 for those who really want to get enthusiastic). However, the basic principle is the same. Almost all the words are sung on one note, called the reciting note. In all tones (other than *recto tono*), there is a bit of variation at the end of the line. This variation is the characteristic melody. Even if you don't know this melody, if you are in a congregation where Vespers is being sung, you can join in the part that is on one note.

Once you have mastered singing on one note, you can probably contemplate the simple tones. We'll come to that later.

FOR THOSE WHO CAN SING ALONG WITH OTHERS, BUT ARE TOO TIMID TO LEAD

This is the category that I belonged to. I knew that I could sing along with others and enjoyed singing. I would sing along with the chants if a choir was leading in church; I would sing at soccer games; I would sing in the bar with the team after playing sports. But I couldn't imagine leading anything.

When I realized that I had to be the one at Thomas More College to lead the singing, I knew this had to change. This is how I got over this hurdle (in fact, it was quite easy): I realized that, paradoxically, the way to feel at ease singing in front of others was to sing on my own. The same exercise that helped me to start singing in tune — singing loudly in the shower and getting used to the sound of my own voice — helped me here too. I found that once I was comfortable listening to my own voice when singing loudly, it didn't seem to make that much difference if others were listening too. It seemed no more unnerving than talking to somebody.

HOW TO SING THE PSALMS

This is something that you can spend years learning and never feel that you master. All I am trying to do here is to give you something that will enable you to begin, so that you can work with your family or another group to learn to sing when you pray the psalms together if you like.

As with all matters of prayer, we want to aim for the highest, because this is something that we are offering up to God. However, as in all matters of prayer, if we can't do something perfectly, we do the best we can anyway.

If you can find someone who is accustomed to singing the psalms, ask to be included. The best way to learn is by imitation. I think that our brethren in the Eastern Church are ahead of us in praying with the family. I have heard several Eastern Catholic and Orthodox families sing night prayers; the psalms are sung simply, usually *recto tono*, led by the father. (If you know such a family, ask if you can join them one night. Notice how easily and happily the children will take their turns at singing on their own.)

A number of things struck me about the way they sing the psalms. First, it is very simple. Slight modulations came to them naturally — otherwise they keep to one note. Each member of the family seems very happy to sing all the psalms in one or two notes, all sounding pretty good to me.

The second thing that struck me about their singing is their simple, unaffected approach. It makes sense. The psalms or any other sacred text will communicate the truths they contain through the words. Just as when reading it in church, I should be content to articulate them clearly: there is no need to inject any emotion or try to act out parts, nor do I need to try to sound pious as I am doing it.

SLOWER IS NOT HOLIER; SILENCE IS GOLDEN

Another point that I noticed about Eastern-rite chanting is that the tempo is a normal talking pace. Most communities that sing the psalms daily that I have heard, whether in English, Arabic, or Latin, go at a much faster pace than you might expect. Actually, a good tempo is traditional to Gregorian chant as well. The principle is to chant at the speed that you would speak.

One reason is that some lines are long, and you need to get through them in a single breath. But another is that there are pauses between lines that impregnate the prayer with meditative silence.

This is something that the Church in the West today has all but lost—the value of silence. At first, the pause between lines seems unnaturally long, so unaccustomed are we to any silence, no matter how short. But soon we notice how poignant the pauses are, especially as the chant before and after is sung at a natural but brisk pace. So, on the one hand, it is not so fast that you sound as though you are commenting on a horse race. On the other, you don't want it so slow that it gives the impression of an affected piety and tries everyone's patience.

LET'S START SINGING

So let's pick the shortest psalm and start singing. Here is Psalm 117:

Praise the Lord, all nations!
Extol him, all peoples!
For great is his steadfast love toward us;
    and the faithfulness of the Lord
    endures for ever.
Praise the Lord!

First of all, read it out loud to yourself.

Now try saying it out loud, but on one note. If you have done this, you have sung it *recto tono*.

You will have had to pause and take breaths at various places. In order to help us do this with others, we set it out according to the natural breaks in the flow of the text.

*Praise the Lord, all nations!**
Extol him, all peoples!

*For great is his steadfast love toward us;**
and the faithfulness of the Lord
endures for ever. Praise the Lord!

You will notice that we have broken the psalm up into two couplets to allow for what is called antiphonal singing, meaning that the group is divided into two, either in two evenly sized groups (say, men and women) or cantor (say, Dad) and everybody else.

Then each side alternates, so the first sings the first couplet and the second group sings the second. The chant swings between the two. It is a dialogue, both active and receptive.

And why the asterisk?

It might seem normal to you that there is a pause between couplets, but that is actually not the best way to chant. The beautiful contemplative moment of silence comes at the asterisk.

So it goes like this: one group (for our purposes, let's say the women) begins, chanting up to the asterisk, and takes a pause (and a breath). Then they finish the couplet. The men immediately, with no pause, enter, taking up their line, then pause in the same way at their asterisk. The momentum swings immediately. If a person finds chant boring or tedious, it is likely because this rhythm isn't followed.

All the traditional psalm tones (that is, tunes) are simple two-line melodies that are repeated to fit texts organized in couplets. In Psalm 117, there are only two couplets because it is so short, but other psalms are much longer. You would just go on singing the same tune many times over, one side yielding to the other, until you have finished. Most tunes are different in the first line and the second, although in the simplest, *recto tono*, we don't see this because everything is sung on the same note.

PSALMS AND CANTICLES

Some breviaries set the psalms out for singing in this way, but some don't. Now that you can see what to do, you can go through with a pencil and mark it up so that it is divided up into couplets (you might have the odd triplet if the number of lines in the psalm is odd). Then you can sing any psalm antiphonally (back and forth if you have more than one person) in *recto tono*. So now, just knowing this one tone, you can sing every psalm, canticle, and hymn!

FOR THOSE WHO WANT TO DO MORE

If you want to sing more, then you should. If you go to my website, http://thewayofbeauty.org, in the section "Psalm Tones" you will find links to videos telling you how. There is an instructional video telling you how to mark the psalms so you can sing them using any of the tones. This is called pointing. Pointing tells the singer which note to apply to which syllable so that groups of people can sing in unison. There is a small selection of tones that you can learn and use.

The advantage for the system of pointing that we use is that, unlike others, it is the same for all the psalms. This enables you always to sing the whole psalter whether you know one or 120 tones. In other psalters, every psalm is assigned its own tone and pointing; there is very little, if any, interchangeability. This is frustrating until you know all the tones in the selection. This is why we recommend the St. Thomas More Primer (see resources) for singing of the psalms.

SINGING THE PSALMS IS AN ORAL TRADITION, NOT A WRITTEN TRADITION

You might not get much further than singing psalms *recto tono* from this instruction alone, but don't be despondent. You are like the majority of people; chant, for the most part, is best learned by listening and doing. It is an oral tradition. In the ideal world, there would be a group near you that you could join in and sing with, such as a monastery or church schola.

If you do not have personal contact with someone who can help you (with this or any other chant system), then organize a group of enthusiasts—perhaps a cluster of families from your parish or neighborhood. I will be happy to try to help. Contact me through the website www.SophiaInstitute.com/LittleOratory.

SINGING THE PARTS OTHER THAN THE PSALMS AND CANTICLES

All the other parts of the Liturgy of the Hours can be intoned or read as seems appropriate. Even the Scripture readings can be sung in one tone.

Hymns

I won't go into singing what most people think of as hymns, but I would like to mention that the *St. Thomas More Primer* has a great selection of Ambrosian hymns. These are written so that they all scan identically. This means that, as with the psalms, once you know one tune, you can sing every hymn to that tune; and as you gradually increase your repertoire of melodies, you can apply them to every hymn.

How to sing as part of a congregation in a choir or following a cantor

Choral singing is a refined art. But even the untutored can join in congregational singing or bring together a group to sing pleasingly with just a few thoughts in mind.

A unified, pure voice with clear, natural, unaffected tones is the goal in singing sacred music. Vibrato is part of good operatic singing, of course, but in choral singing, the vibrato must be kept discreet, never drawing attention to itself. Learning to use the breath with relaxation will prevent straining the voice, which isn't good for any style of singing. The key is to use the breath from the diaphragm, not any tightening of the vocal cords, to produce the sound.

Unifying with others around us requires the virtue of humility. We must be prepared to blend with others and not stand out. Very often, this is a greater problem in church congregations with confident singers who perhaps feel that the onus is on them to lead the inexperienced or who have just never considered the importance of listening to and blending with those around them. Even the choir and the cantor should strive for an unaffected style of singing that is nevertheless very beautiful.

The following story indicates that even when the whole congregation knows the music intimately, the result can be disunity:

When I was at the Sacra Liturgia 2013 conference in Rome, a meeting of those (mostly clerics and religious, apart from me) interested in the Liturgy, we had two Latin Masses and two Solemn Vespers, all with a wonderful choir leading the congregation in chant. This was a congregation that knew their chant. Many were experienced in leading and teaching. I would suppose that all there were in agreement that Latin is the norm for the Mass and that chant and polyphony are the highest forms in which to sing it. Not surprisingly, many people joined in with the choir at the conference Liturgy.

What was surprising, given the company, was how the congregational members (which included me until I noticed my fault) failed to unify their voices with each other and the choir. Some around me were singing so loudly and obtrusively that I could barely hear myself, let alone the choir, sing. How, I wondered, could these people possibly be listening to others and blending while singing at that volume? Individually we knew the music, but we really were a fragmented collection of individuals, so much so that one of the speakers — a Benedictine monk — later remarked upon it.

I resolved actually to follow the advice I have been giving you in this book: that is, to sing at a volume at which I could hear myself *and* the others. Then I just trusted that this was loud enough to be adding to the general volume of the unified voice.

The other difficulty at the conference was trying to start each line at the same time. The choir sang antiphonally with a large pause between the lines of each couplet. People didn't know precisely when they were supposed to start singing again. Some tried to anticipate, jumping in when they thought it was the right time. Some sang early, causing a blurred rather than a precise start. Some came in late and then accelerated through the next few words to try to catch up. As a result, we couldn't make out the words clearly. I resolved to listen for the first syllable sung by the choir and then join in on the second in unison with the choir. This way it didn't disrupt the rhythm of the psalm. It would allow for a crisp, clear beginning to each line. (If you can see the choir director's movements, then you will know exactly when to start, because he will indicate the moment.)

FORMATION IN BEAUTY

It has since struck me how singing in a choir and aiming for a beautiful unified voice requires us to think about the three aspects of beauty described by St. Thomas Aquinas: due proportion, integrity, and clarity. This is why learning to sing in unison will form us very deeply in an understanding of beauty.

Here's how:

• *Due proportion* means that within the thing being considered, each part is in right relationship to the others—the parts sit harmoniously together. We see this in chant when we sing in unison. We must sing the same rhythm and tone. The singer must listen to the voices of those around him so that his voice will blend. Even if he knows the piece perfectly, he cannot blend with the others unless he considers how his voice relates to the unified voice of the choir.

• *Integrity* is the degree to which the whole thing conforms to its purpose. In a choir, even beyond the choice of the music and the words, there has to be a consideration of interpretation. The director must decide upon an interpretation that all subscribe to. It would be hopeless if each singer interpreted individually and then sang accordingly. We must accept the authority of the leader to direct that unified voice to a purpose that is appropriate to the choir (this is also a good exercise in humility!).

• *Clarity* can be thought of as the radiance of truth. For something to be beautiful, it must communicate clearly what it is. So in this context it means a clear articulation of the words and music with the unity of one voice, an awareness of the meaning (interpretation and integrity), and being heard by others. And, ultimately, God hears us sing with the heart of prayer.

All these things are essential, I would suggest, when we sing in the Liturgy ... and are probably a good idea everywhere else too!

Appendix H

Natural Wonders at the Prayer Table

by Leila Marie Lawler

Today many families arrive at the idea of the family altar by way of the nature table in the Montessori or Waldorf style of education. The nature table is a place in the home where children can display and ponder those little objects from nature they are always picking up on their walks. Since these objects are endlessly fascinating, enriching, and interesting, the idea is that this way, the child can return to them, handle them, think about them, and learn more about them at his own pace. At the same time, the objects are centralized and don't become so much trash in the house, forgotten and no longer enchanting.

You might want to place the nature table by the door where you enter from the walk. That way, the child can immediately take the things he has collected out of his pockets or his bag and arrange them. Over and over, people familiar with this practice of the nature table have been impressed with the child's ability not only to organize the things he has collected, but also to arrange them with a lot of delight and attractiveness.

The Psalms tell us of the wonders of God's creation and the goodness of the things He has put in the world.

The earth is the Lord's and the fullness thereof: the world, and all they that dwell therein. (Ps 24:1)

Come and behold ye the works of the Lord: what wonders he hath done upon earth. (Ps. 45:9, Douay-Rheims; RSV: 46:8)

How great are thy works, O Lord? Thou hast made all things in wisdom: the earth is filled with thy riches. (Ps. 103:24, Douay-Rheims; RSV: 104:24)

The heaven of heaven is the Lord's: but the earth he has given to the children of men. (Ps. 113:24, Douay-Rheims; RSV: 115:16)

And so on.

To a child, a seashell—even a not particularly nice one, from a grown-up's point of view—is a miracle. And so it is.

To integrate this real gift of wonder at nature that children experience with the spiritual wonder that happens at the prayer table, you might consider placing there a small dish of some kind. We all have some lone shallow dish, basket, or bowl—perhaps a saucer from a long-ago broken set—that would be perfect to place on or near the prayer table. Then the child can pick a choice specimen from the nature table—a pinecone, a little smooth rock, a bit of moss, a pearly shell—and place it as a decoration on the home altar.

As with the flowers, as discussed in chapter 3, the children can be the curators of this aspect of the oratory. Encourage them to retire something that has lost its appeal or is out of season. Keep this activity strictly limited to what can fit on the dish. And occasionally clean the dish!

RESOURCES FOR PRAYER LIFE IN THE HOME

We want to continue to encourage you to pray—and to unite your prayer to that of our Holy Mother Church. This list of resources is intentionally quite limited: we are aware of the vast riches of our Faith and have enumerated a few things that have been useful to us. We think they will be useful to you too. We trust that the Holy Spirit will lead you to what you need from here, without our burdening you with a vast reading list.

On our websites, we have many more suggestions for living your faith in the home, in church, and in the world.

David's site: http://thewayofbeauty.org.

Leila's site: www.likemotherlikedaughter.org.

LIVING THE LITURGICAL YEAR

When it's united with the Sacred Liturgy, family life is ideally suited to bringing up children in the Faith. For a comprehensive guide to saints, feasts, fasts, and activities, see the "Liturgical Year" page at the Catholic Culture website (www.catholicculture.org).

Once you have the idea of the prayer table and the Liturgy of the Hours, Mary Reed Newland's books will give you many ways to expand your home celebration of the liturgical calendar. See especially *We and Our Children* and *The Year and Our Children*.

CATECHISM

For adults

In the old *Baltimore Catechism*, children learned that we are here to "know God, to love him …" When we think about it, we must know in order to love!

We direct you to the vast treasury of the *Catechism of the Catholic Church*. Not only does it contain the Church's basic teachings on faith and morals, but it is written in a way that will enrich study and prayer. Dip in, of course (and it can be found and searched online), for immediate answers to burning questions; for greatest effect, also try reading it from the beginning—we suggest ten or fifteen minutes at a time. It's a book to come back to again and again.

For children

We hope our book has demonstrated how a lived faith in the family is its own catechesis —that is, how one can learn more about God just by living life along with His Church, at home. To understand the delicacy required to transmit the Faith to children when we seek to teach them directly, see Sofia Cavalletti's *The Religious Potential of the Child: Experiencing Scripture and Liturgy with Young Children.*

Catechesis of the Good Shepherd (The Atrium) is a Montessori-based religion program for children developed by Sofia Cavalletti and can be found at www.cgsusa.org. This program revolves around the liturgical year and is thus a boon to parents. We recommend it with slight reservations regarding the presentation of material for older children, but when used in conjunction with the *Catechism of the Catholic Church* (as a resource for a parent or teacher) and the *Baltimore Catechism* (as an outline for teaching children), its scriptural approach will be a great benefit.

The New Saint Joseph Baltimore Catechism series, by Bennet Kelley, while no longer on the bishops' approved list of catechetical texts for *classrooms*, will always be an important resource for parents needing a systematic approach to teaching faith and morals to children. It includes the important prayers for children to learn.

For older children who might not be ready for the *Catechism of the Catholic Church*, you will find *Youcat*, edited by Christoph Schönborn, useful.

For parents looking for a guide to speaking to children about sacred things, we recommend Maria Montessori's *The Mass Explained to Children*, from Kessenger Legacy Reprints. Although Montessori speaks in this book of the Extraordinary Form of the Mass, the meditations are applicable to helping a child understand the elements of any Liturgy.

BREVIARIES

To pray the Liturgy of the Hours with the universal Church, consider one of these options:

For a one-volume version, look for *Shorter Christian Prayer* from Catholic Book Publishing (also known as *Christian Prayer: The Liturgy of the Hours*, from the Daughters of St. Paul, which it temporarily out of print).

For the complete, multivolume version, you can purchase *Liturgy of the Hours*, from Catholic Book Publishing (in the United States), or the *Divine Office*, from Harper Collins (in the United Kingdom and the Commonwealth).

Steve Cavanaugh's *St. Thomas More Primer* is a daily office book intended for the Ordinariate of the Chair of St. Peter and other U.S. Catholics of Anglican heritage but is a suitable resource for any Catholic not bound to a particular form. This Breviary includes prayers for many occasions and can be spoken or chanted, alone or in a group, using David's methods for the amateur or beginner musician (see www. thomasmoreprimer.com).

Online or downloadable versions of the Liturgy of the Hours are available at: iBreviary (www.ibreviary.org); DivineOffice.org (http://divineoffice.org); and Universalis (http://universalis.com).

Magnificat, available by yearly subscription, is a monthly missal for Mass that also offers an abbreviated Liturgy of the Hours. With beautiful art and excellent reflections, it is well worth the price: www.magnificat.com.

General Instruction of the Liturgy of the Hours, an overview and instruction printed at the beginning of some Breviaries, can be found online at www.ewtn.com/library/curia/cdwgilh.htm.

For further instruction on praying the Liturgy of the Hours, see Daria Sockey, *The Everyday Catholic's Guide to the Liturgy of the Hours*.

For a compilation of prayers and devotions, check your Breviary. We also recommend *The Handbook of Prayers*, by James Socias.

SCRIPTURE

Every home needs a good and beautiful translation of the Bible (preferably for each person in the house!).

We recommend the *Ignatius Bible*, published by Ignatius Press. This is the Revised Standard Version, translated in beautiful modern language without concession to political correctness or theological dumbing down.

For a study bible, we recommend the *Ignatius Catholic Study Bible*, compiled and edited by Curtis Mitch and Scott Hahn, respectively; also the *Navarre Bible*, published by University of Navarre.

For deep and invigorating Scripture studies in a group, we recommend those offered by the Catholic Scripture Study International; www.cssprogram.net.

For children
We encourage you not to be afraid to read to children from actual Scripture — especially the parables of Jesus. This is the method of the Catechesis of the Good Shepherd (noted earlier), which in turn reaches back to the way children were originally taught before there was the thought of religion classes or specialized books directed at children.

However, a children's Bible can help familiarize little ones with the beloved Bible stories, provided that the text doesn't stray too far from or introduce elements not present in the original. We also urge you to be attentive to the illustrations and overall way the book is made. Avoid anything undignified or ugly!

Fr. Lawrence G. Lovasik's *New Catholic Picture Bible* takes care to show how the the New Testament is foreshadowed in the Old.

365 Bible Stories and Verses, by Muriel Granger, from Golden Press, is out of print but available second-hand.

Hurlbut's *Story of the Bible* is available from different publishers and online for free at the Baldwin Online Children's Literature Project: www.mainlesson.com. This story Bible was written by a Methodist in 1904 and has remained a beloved favorite. It emphasizes important points in salvation history, making it helpful for teaching God's action in the history of His people.

For a good Scripture study program for students right before high school, we recommend *The Great Adventure* Bible timeline study called T3 (although we would love to see it presented with more beauty). You can find it at http://biblestudyforcatholics.com/bible-study-world/.

VATICAN DOCUMENTS

Our Church is indeed a treasury of wisdom, passed down to us through the centuries, ever new for the next generation. Although sometimes a bit difficult to read, this treasury rewards inquiry. An important point to remember: when you read a document, be aware that it will always refer to (even if not explicitly) and be united with the documents that preceded it, most importantly, Sacred Scripture. The lineage of any teaching can be traced in the footnotes of the given document.

For a full list of papal and other documents that form part of the Magisterium (teaching role) of the Catholic Church, visit the Catholic Culture website: www.catholicculture.org/culture/library. You can also search the Vatican website: www.vatican.va/archive/index.htm.

For the purposes of inquiring more into what the Church teaches about the importance of family life in the Christian home, we especially recommend *Familiaris Consortio* (The Role of the Christian Family in the Modern World), an apostolic exhortation of John Paul II.

To read about the Eucharist, Sunday worship, and beauty, try the apostolic exhortation of Benedict XVI called *Sacramentum Caritatis*.

For guidance on music in the Liturgy, read *Musicum Sacram*, Vatican II's Instruction for Music.

BEAUTY IN ART AND MUSIC IN THE LITURGY

On this topic, we recommend Pope Benedict XVI's *Spirit of the Liturgy* and Jean Corbon's *The Wellspring of Worship*, both from Ignatius Press, and Scott Hahn's *Letter and Spirit: From Written Text to Living Word in the Liturgy*, from Doubleday.

Paul Jernberg's *The Logos of Sacred Music* can be found at www.catholicculture.org/commentary/articles.cfm?id=535. Jernberg's music for the new translation of the English Mass, The Mass of St. Philip Neri, can be found at www.csmus.org.

Adoremus, a society for the renewal of the Sacred Liturgy, can be found online at www.adoremus.org.

Acknowledgments

I would especially like thank the following for their help and guidance over many years: Robert Clayton, Stratford Caldecott, Caroline Farey, Tom Larson, Shawn Tribe, Aidan Hart, William Fahey, and Stephen Cavanaugh; and Leila for her patience and perseverance.

—*David Clayton*

Thanks first of all must go to David Clayton, for inviting me to join him in the writing of this book. David's generosity and clear understanding cannot be praised enough.

My family has taught me how to live the life of the Church in the home. My husband, Phil, with his great faith and encouragement, and my children, with their sweet, open wonder, have brought me with them on this journey of love that is our family.

My daughter Rosie Turner started our blog, Like Mother, Like Daughter, which has been my outlet until now for expressing my thoughts on what liturgical life in the home is all about. I thank her for her encouragement. My daughter Suzanne Saur was invaluable in reading this manuscript with her sharp eye for meaning. I'm also very grateful that they each know so much about music.

And, of course, my daughter Deirdre Folley contributed the drawings throughout, without which the text would lack liveliness and a visual expression of the holy homiic we are trying to convey. Her husband, John, provided excellent support as she worked on the many illustrations while welcoming their new baby, Evangeline Rose, into the world.

My sons, Nick, Joseph, and William, always provide encouragement and a sense of appreciation, without which a mother can hardly dare to encourage others. Nick's wife, Natasha, was enthusiastic about the idea of a book about the home altar. Our conversations about what she has encountered in her travels helped me gain insight into how to present our Catholic tradition.

My youngest daughter, Bridget, fairly ran our home in the most cheerful way possible while I immersed myself in the work of this book. As always, my mother, Elizabeth Edwards, simply gives me what every daughter needs: unconditional affirmation.

When it comes to the little oratory in the home, my friends Therese Cross and Susan Nohrden helped this convert see tradition better. Therese's example of passing along what she has received from her Catholic heritage in her manner of making her home, and Sue's great dedication to the Atrium (the Catechesis of the Good Shepherd) have both been formative for me. It was due to Sue's determination to spread the word of liturgical living in the home in our parish that I was moved to send an outline of my ideas to David, with whom I've had a meeting of minds since we met a few years ago; and it was thus that he realized we were working on essentially the same idea, from different approaches.

For his insight into the liturgy and music, his beautiful compositions, and his willingness to share his gifts with his friends, Paul Jernberg has my gratitude.

My dear friends Erin Conner, Christina Wassell, and Ann and Ted Turner contributed with their thoughts and intelligent readings of the manuscript.

—*Leila Marie Lawler*

ABOUT THE AUTHORS

DAVID CLAYTON

David Clayton is an internationally known artist, teacher, writer, and broadcaster. He holds a faculty position as Artist-in-Residence and Lecturer in Liberal Arts at Thomas More College of Liberal Arts, in Merrimack, New Hampshire.

David moved to the United States from his native England in January 2009 to take up his current position. Before moving to the United States he taught at the Maryvale Institute, Birmingham, England, where he designed, along with the staff at the institute, their art-theory course: Art, Beauty, and Inspiration from a Catholic Perspective. This course is offered in the United States via the diocese of Kansas City, Kansas, and David teaches the residential weekends there.

His artistic training is both in the sacred art tradition of Byzantine iconography and as a portrait painter in the style of Western classical naturalism, which he studied in Florence, Italy. Aside from the work he is currently doing for the Thomas More College chapel, major commissions include: St. Luigi Scrosoppi, for the London Oratory; the five-foot Crucifixion at Pluscarden Monastery in Elgin, Scotland; and the Sacred Heart at Maryvale Institute. His work has been featured in the UK national daily newspapers the *Guardian* and the *Times*.

David wrote, co-produced, and presented *The Way of Beauty*, a thirteen-part TV series about traditional art and culture shown on Catholic TV in 2010 and 2011.

He has illustrated a number of children's books published in the United Kingdom and in the United States, including collaborations with Scott Hahn and a book on devotion to the Sacred Heart of Jesus with Cardinal Burke, Prefect of the Supreme Tribunal of the Apostolic Signatura. David writes for his weekly blog, The Way of Beauty, http://thewayofbeauty.org, and is the sacred-art writer for the highly influential and widely read New Liturgical Movement website, www.newliturgicalmovement.org.

David was received into the Church in London in 1993.

(David Clayton is sole owner of the service mark and trademark The Way of Beauty.)

LEILA MARIE LAWLER

Leila Marie Lawler is a wife of one, mother of seven, and grandmother of four (and counting), living in central Massachusetts.

Leila encountered Christianity as a high school student and entered the Catholic Church in 1979, the year she married Philip Lawler, a noted Catholic journalist.

Her own journey of learning the Faith has given her an appreciation for the difficulties and excitement today's family faces in living its Christian calling. She encourages audiences of all kinds to commit to the renewal of family life.

Leila practices "kitchen-sink philosophy" at Like Mother, Like Daughter (www.like-motherlikedaughter.org), a website offering practical and theoretical insight into all aspects of daily life. She writes on everything from cooking and knitting to education and recovering what she and her daughters call "the collective memory."

DEIRDRE M. FOLLEY

Deirdre M. Folley contributed the illustrations for this book from her home in the Washington, DC, metro area, around the time that she and her husband, artist John Folley, welcomed their firstborn child. Deirdre's pursuits, from the practical and the artistic to the theoretical and intellectual, are varied, but all converge at her interest in and passion for Catholic culture and the good of marriage and the family. Primarily instructed in art by her grandmother, Elizabeth Edwards, Deirdre also studied art under John Schmitt, son of artist Carl Schmitt, as well as at the Catholic University of America, where she majored in philosophy.

NOTES

NOTES

NOTES

NOTES

An Invitation

Reader, the book that you hold in your hands was published by Sophia Institute Press. Sophia Institute seeks to nurture the spiritual, moral, and cultural life of souls and to spread the Gospel of Christ in conformity with the authentic teachings of the Roman Catholic Church.

Our press fulfills this mission by offering translations, reprints, and new publications that afford readers a rich source of the enduring wisdom of mankind.

We also operate two popular online Catholic resources: CrisisMagazine.com and CatholicExchange.com.

Crisis Magazine provides insightful cultural analysis that arms readers with the arguments necessary for navigating the ideological and theological minefields of the day. *Catholic Exchange* provides world news from a Catholic perspective as well as daily devotionals and articles that will help you to grow in holiness and live a life consistent with the teachings of the Church.

Sophia Institute Press also serves as the publisher for the Thomas More College of Liberal Arts and Holy Spirit College. Both colleges provide university-level education under the guiding light of Catholic teaching. If you know a young person seeking a college that takes seriously the adventure of learning and the quest for truth, please bring these institutions to his attention.

www.SophiaInstitute.com
www.CatholicExchange.com
www.CrisisMagazine.com

Sophia Institute Press® is a registered trademark of Sophia Institute.
Sophia Institute is a tax-exempt institution as defined by the
Internal Revenue Code, Section 501(c)(3). Tax I.D. 22-2548708.

THE VISITATION